Om, to the ultimate result of the good!

The Contract of the Soul
Revised Edition © 2011

A message about humanity's spiritual evolution

Rev. Rina A. González

The Contract of the Soul
Revised Edition © 2011
A message about humanity's spiritual evolution

ISBN # **978-0-9792408-2-9**

Self Published in the U.S.A.
By, Rev. Rina A. González

Contact Information:

        E-mail :   rina@angelicgoddesses.com
        Web Site: http://www.angelicgoddesses.com

Copyright © 2011

     All rights are reserved by the author. No part of this publication may be reproduced, stored in a retrieval system, or transmitted in any form or by any other mean whether, electronic, mechanical, photocopy or recorded, without the prior written permission of the author.

Dedication

I dedicate this book to the five most important people in my life; my parents and my three children. My parents, for giving me the will to be, and my children, for being the constant reminder that I needed to grow.

To all of you goes my undying love!

Index

Prepare for Destiny's Call (Poem)	13
To my Father (Poem)	15
Introduction	19
Dual Nature	27
My Parents	30
1944, Year of the Wood Monkey	34
As My World Turned	37
References	42
The Visit	49
The Invitation	53
This Thing Called Life (Poem)	57
Accepting the Invitation	59
Do what's in your nature (Poem)	67
Awakening	70
Gratitude	75
Life is a Dance: Dance it!	77
Non-Acceptance	81
To Live Again {Poem}	89
Working the Soul Contract	93
Inspirational Thoughts	97
Playing the Game of Life	99
Voyage to the Unknown	103
Unveiling Life's Mysteries	107
Parents Soul Contract	111
The relationship between mother and child	115
The contract between siblings	121
Soul Mates	125
Best Friend	127
To be happy, find your passion….	131
The perfection in what's strange	132

Places and Things	135
To err is divine {Poem}	137
Planet Earth	139
Womanhood	143
Life is a Choice	147
Alpha and Omega (Poem)	151
Final Thoughts	153

A human being is a part of the whole called by us "the universe," a part limited in time and space. He experiences himself, his thoughts and feelings, as something separate from the rest ~ a kind of optical delusion of consciousness. This delusion is a kind of prison for us, restricting us to our personal desires and affections for a few persons nearest to us. Our task must be to free ourselves from this prison by widening the circle of understanding and compassion to embrace all living creatures and the whole of nature in its beauty.

Albert Einstein

"Man's only obligation in life is to comply with his personal legacy. In obtaining clarity of mind man is lead to find his purpose and in obeying spirit's call is that he is lead to find the key to his own emancipation."

Rev. Rina

The highest thoughts are those thoughts which contain joy, the clearest words are those words which contain truth, the grandest feeling is that feeling which we call love. Joy, Truth, Love - these three are interchangeable it matters not which appears first...

Neale Donald Walsch

Prepare for Destiny's Call!

(Prepara bien tu destino)
To my daughter, Rina

From the depth of your embrace
I see the world through your eyes.
Don't forget to plan ahead
Prepare for destiny's plan.

Get ready for what's to come
Do not fear asking why.
Always give and seek respect
And welcome a guiding hand.

Teachers and divine books
Will always be by your side.
They will open many doors
That will take you to your path.

Trust in what you have learned,
Allow your spirit to soar
By accepting what life brings,
Life's wonders you will discover.

Author, Albino H. González Montesinos
1916-1958
Written in Queens, N.Y. in 1956
Translated by: Rina A. González in 2005

Rev. Rina A. González

To My Father
Albino H. González Montesinos

It would not be fair if I did not try
Writing a poem to your undying love.
I have your ideas and love for rhymes;
It would seem illogical if I did not try.

Although I know deep in my heart
That destiny had my life planed out,
Yet, to your memory, I'll take pen in hand
And write some words that I will call mine.

Knowing that they are more than simple words
For I hold your memory close to my heart.
Yet, see that the more I try to write at will
The less that the rhymes came into the screen.

So I will do what I know so well,
Allow your memory to come, to evolve.
As your essence appears, the words will flow
From my heart to the paper, creating a poem.

Little did I know when I was a child
That our relationship was preordained.
It is surreal to see that you knew
What my fate was to be, before it came true.

What you saw me doing when I was a child
I could not have imagined it could ever be,
For I must admit that the words I write
Are guided in faith and dressed in sunlight.

Rev. Rina A. González

You left me too soon; you were very young.
Yet, I could see that your spirit was old.
For you knew what I held and what was to be.
You are one of the angels that gave me my wings.

You showed to be generous and kind
By guiding me to see the soul within life.
And to my amazement, you gave me the wisdom,
Of how to be on purpose and how to be real.

I am humble to have known you and that we were friends.
I am glad that we choose love to conquer our fate.
Yours was to guide me, mine is to provide
The world with a message that's deep in my heart.

In this, our relationship of father and daughter
I see that we have triumph and at last are free.
We were there for each other when all else failed,
I held to my beginnings, and my dream prevailed.

For I see that love holds the key to life,
This is who we are, and what we'll always be.
Your teachings are with me each and every day.
I hold them to the light and I'm shown the way.

You are in my heart in more ways than one.
Thank you for the blessings and for your embrace.
Thanks for believing in my deepest wish.
Today I am wiser, and know that I am free!

To your loving memory!

The Contract of the Soul ~ Revised Edition 2011

Rev. Rina A. González

Love, Light and Laughter are powerful energies, capable of changing any situation in your life.

Love is what you are; embrace it! Light comes from the soul, shine on! Laughter is a great healer of the seen and the unseen alike!

Together, this great equalizer has the capacity to shift the body's energy from dense to light, transforming any imperfection and turning back the hands of time.

Learn to value these three wonderful gifts of the soul. Use them consciously, and in time, you will be rewarded with the perfection of wholeness in mind, body, and soul.

Rev. Rina

Introduction

*...although, they wish for happiness,
out of ignorance, they destroy it like a foe.*

Buddhist Master Shantideva

Life is simple; too simple perhaps. Reason why, its' truest essence escapes us. As I look around see that out of what is beautiful and simple, humanity has managed to complicate by not understanding that our lives can be better by learning to use the powers of the soul correctly.

Yes! I believe that if we dared to look beyond what social condition dictates and allowed the soul to take its rightful place in our lives, we not only would benefit our lives, but also, we would influence the state of our world.

What I give you in this book is something so simple that anyone can do it. You do not need a PhD to achieve spiritual growth. All that is required of you is that you have an open mind and are willing to do the work required, in doing so you will reach the highest pinnacle in your spiritual awakening. What I give you works, because it addresses our deepest truth. And it works best if you are real with yourself and dare ask the tough questions of yourself and of life, especially when it comes to something as important as your own spirituality.

For instance, it might come in handy to know that *'we'*, all souls having a physical experience have signed a contract, prior to our arrival on Planet Earth, in every one of our incarnations, agreeing to learning, evolving, and growing. However, because of not knowing our deepest truth, for eons, humanity has turned learning a lesson, into a problem, creating something negative out of what is meant to empower the individual.

Misunderstanding a lesson and calling 'a lesson' 'a problem' comes from ignoring who you are and what you are here to do. Many have gotten used to *'the way things are'* and dare not change or correct the incorrect information of ourselves, of others and of life. Not knowing that through our perception is that life is lived, or that perception is a spiritual gift, many live life incorrectly.

Anytime incorrect information is perceived about 'something or someone', this misperception is what is stored in the mind, in the subconscious and in the memory cells of the body, and from this misconception is that you live your life and is the only thing you have to give yourself and others.

What is more letting is that from this diluted version of the self is how life is created by those individuals who do not know how powerful they truly are, yet dare to blame 'anyone around them' for not having reached the life they think they deserve.

The good that you seek seldom goes your way, because of your inability to reason that you are the architect of your destiny. To fix what is wrong find the flaws in your personality and make sure that your thoughts, words, and actions resonate to the quality of life you want to have.

Humanity's behavior defines the meaning of insanity to perfection. According to *Albert Einstein*, insanity is doing the same thing over and over again expecting a different result."

Because of humanity's arrogance and ignorance and by force of habit we have become accustomed to calling ourselves what we are not and repeatedly do the same things that bring us what we do not want to experience. In our absence from our lives, our true essence, our soul, has never taken its rightful place in any of our earthly experience{s}; making this the greatest travesty of them all.

The reason why humanity has not evolved, as it should have, it's because, for generations we have used the wrong information, repeatedly. In every live, the incorrect information has been stored in the mind, in the sub-conscious and in our cells, making our misunderstandings and misconceptions habitual in nature, thus they have crystallized. This crystallization makes change hard and sometimes and impossible feat. Make mo mistake about this, from these harness of mind [crystallization], the imperfection of thought has been affirmed and these imperfections are what inevitably, will materialize in your life.

This imperfect state of being, is present in today's world. If you doubt the validity of this statement, look around you. For many of us, this incorrect information is 'the norm' and what we fear most is changing that which has the power to destroy us. These outdated customs creates unhealthy behavior. And this mind stuff is what rules our lives; showing that Pete and Repeat are alive and well. Unless humanity is willing to change, by learning a new way of living life, we will keep on making the same poor choices that can only bring us the same unwanted results.

In the absence of logic, our lives have become what they were never supposed to be, a burden. As a result, and in the absent from our lives, decay and disorder are present in everything we think say and do. For far too long, human behavior has become unreasonable, unruly and has deteriorated, yet we have stood idle in the hopes that 'a cure all' would come our way. Perhaps, this cure would come in the form of a pill that can do for us what we have not been able to do for ourselves. Which of course, to date has not happened, nor will it ever take place.

After years of ignoring our truth and in the absence of logic, humanity has managed to destroy entire species from the face of our planet. Entire lifetimes have been lived without having experienced love or compassion. Then again, how can love or compassion be part of the person who lacks loving or caring for himself or herself self? This is what has caused devastation and destruction to many life forms on Planet Earth.

Do not be fooled, if logic, love, and compassion are missing from your life, it is also missing from your home, your family, your work, your neighborhood, your schools, your cities, your towns, your country, and ultimately, it is missing from your world.

I understand that when a person is confused, the last thing in their mind is to reason or that 'a binding document was signed prior to his or hers birth'. However, it was. You should want to know more about how this document works, and how it can help you in your every day life.

Since *the soul contract* is not common knowledge, it tends to reason that this would be the last thing that you or anyone else thinks of or would want to honor. Yet this document should be honored each second that we are alive.

The need to grow, mentally and spiritually, is at hand. Waking up from the sound sleep of the ages is appropriate and doing so will facilitate learning your true value. And this in turn leads you receiving the wisdom of the soul. Only by accepting who and what you are, can you ever hope to evolve. Waiting for a miracle to come and solve your current situation, is not spiritual growth. However, it is stagnation.

You want a miracle. Then be the miracle you want. You are the miracle and the miracle maker. You are the dream and the dreamer and you can make your dreams your reality by learning to work with your spiritual gifts, which have been with you throughout eternity.

Who you are and what you are has been with you in every one of your experiences. Who you are, is part of your genetic and molecular structure. Who you are, is as close to you as the life force that flows through you, for it is you.

Our spiritual side or true nature has become strange to our human experience, as if our reality could be set aside.

Instead of reasoning or understanding what is happening inside and around us, we resort to arguing and making excuses when all we have to do is learn and from learning evolve. When we act in haste, all we have to show is unhappiness, not to mention the waste of precious energy.

Many of us have failed to learn the required lessons in several lifetimes, yet as brave souls keep coming back, in the hopes of getting 'this thing called life' right, to no avail. This has happened because we fail to see that in the absence of wisdom, logic, and reasoning, havoc is present. Yet, how can we understand life, when we do not understand our nature?

The human race has come to 'earth school for the souls' seeking to learn and instead of learning how to make life an adventure for many, life has become a source of disenchantment. We have gotten on the wheel of birth and re-birth {life's merry-go-round}, so many times that it is difficult to remember what we came to do. We have come back in different bodies, have lived in different countries, have come in many shapes, colors, and sizes; yet it seems that nothing has awaken us, long enough to remember that we can break the cycle of birth and rebirth or how to live a karma free existence.

Something else that might interest you to know is that we are born onto the same family nucleus, reason why we should honor those who from generation to generation have had the foresight to advance the family blood line, either through an invention that benefits everyone, or a simple act of kindness that made life kinder and gentler for the immediate family members. And of course, we have also chosen to experienced being either a male or female yet, collectible all we have managed to do is create confusion, devastation, and decay, and this is very different from progress.

Not understanding how to live our lives is the only reason why problem arises. Plain and simple; we are souls in the classroom of life who have forgotten how to be adventurers and have allowed drama {conflict} to mock us, day in and day out. No more and no less!

In our infantile mindset, we struggle against that which has the power to set us free. We contradict that which we do not understand by taking a stance against it. In our ignorance, we try to repress or ignore our own grace by calling it what it is not, expecting to get good results.

Know that the only thing you have created by denying your very truth is that which you do not want to experience. Repeatedly the lessons keep showing up ready to teach you, yet have refused to learn. By not learning, you have stumped your personal growth, have stopped your spiritual potential, have denied yourself having the ability to reason, and your will to survive is in peril.

Humanity in her stupor and unwillingness to grow, has remained loyal to old traditions, and by creating a falsehood of its truth, has endangered its own survival. Between falsehoods, old habits and stupor humanity has remained ignorant of its powers. For many, life instead of being peaceful and harmonious is a constant source of struggle and deprivation. The consequences for this collective ignorance, is having poor health, lack of money and impaired relationships.

So let me ask you. What is life? How do you think life should be lived? What are you personal believes about life? More importantly, who are you? Know that anytime you accept other people's opinions as real, your truth is somewhere in the background, unheard, unexpressed and misunderstood by the very person who can benefit the most. YOU!

It would prove valuable to know that semantics have no value in spirit. The who, the what, the where are unimportant, while receiving the message and learning the lesson(s) it's all that is required. Albert Einstein said it best when he stated, "I want to know the mind of God, the rest are details." And of course, he was right!

Humans get lost in the process of thinking too much and dare call this process reasoning. In doing so, these individuals have missed the essence of life itself. Spirit just **is** and it does not need to prove anything to anyone, or reason what it already *knows is*.

Look at it this way; if you already knew everything, no learning would be required of you and your life would be perfect. The mere fact that you are reading this book proves that you are in the process of evolving and need help understanding how to do it. Getting better at this thing called life starts the moment you make the conscious decision to change.

Let me ask you this;

- How many times has the classroom bell rung to find that you were not ready for class?
- How many entrance exams will you need to take in order to understand how to live your life?
- What needs to happen in order for you to want to be a part of your life?
- When will you hold yourself accountable for having chosen unconsciousness over clarity of mind?
- How many books do you need to read before putting what you have learned into good practice?

Knowledge unless applied properly is rendered useless, turns its holder into an empty vessel and inevitable his emptiness will betray him. My advice, choose to be wise instead.

The Author

Rev. Rina A. González

The Contract of the Soul ~ Revised Edition 2011

Dual Nature

The only animal, who stumbles with the same rock twice, is man!

Synopsis: I AM a soul who has a mind. The soul assures me that, I AM a spark of divinity that has traveled through time and space, assuring me that growth is possible in this incarnation by learning to transcend the limits of the mind. The human mind makes claim only to this. I find myself having come back to the fertile grounds of this beautiful planet as clueless as I was before. However, there is one thing of which I am certain of; I am trying to remember what I have forgotten.

In this lifetime, I chose to be a woman, even remember that as a soul, had this thing called life planned out. So what happened? In all honesty, the mind could not remember what the soul knows, the human side could not understand what was happening or knew how to fix what had become unglued, nor did it listen to the soul's advice.

Because of my confused state of mind, and in the absence of memory, logic, and reasoning, life got rather interesting for me and for those around me. My untrained mind continued creating the same experiences, those I did not want to have, until I finally understand that to have a better life, something needed to change. Tried to change and here again met with the resistance of the untrained mind for while I wanted to change, not knowing what to change or how to change it, was useless.

Allow me to take you back to the beginning of my earthly experience with a narrative that should read, 'my birth was spectacular.' Yes, I was born! To my parents delight a wonder was born, whom they name Rina. I am sure that both my parents were happy with the arrival of their new bundle of joy. I remember the day well; it was a Sunday afternoon, during the summer heat of June 1944 in Havana, Cuba.

I am sure that after my birth someone made sure that my breathing was okay. They even made sure that I had a full set of digits in both, hands and feet, while someone else checked my bodily functions.

The doctor told my parents that that their newborn daughter was normal. The question is, ~ I was normal, compared to what? In those days, the child's blood was not tested for any abnormalities. Since no test was available, my parent's did not know that I was born with the RH-Negative Factor and that in all probability I needed a transfusion.

However, not knowing that anything was wrong with their precious gift, my parent's did the next best thing; ignored what soon would prove to be relevant. Because of the ignorance of our recent history, I was sick most of the time from different things and not until the birth of my third child was I given the remedy to what ailed me.

The remedy was:

- Draw blood intravenously within the first 48 hours of having given birth.
- Send the blood to a lab and turning my blood into a serum.
- Intravenously inject the serum into my blood stream by the third day after having given birth.

The Contract of the Soul ~ Revised Edition 2011

  Fortunately, the process worked and today I am the healthiest I have ever been [as long as I stay away from sunrays or the heat. Childhood was a mixture of gladness and sadness. I was glad when I played with other children and was sad when I could not. Because of my adverse reaction to heat, I could not go out and play with the other children. As you can imagine interaction with others was limited, reason why I could only go out, before sunrise or after sunset. If I went out any other time during the day, my skin would blister.

  Yet, have come to appreciate the hidden blessing of these occurrences, for it was then that I learned the value of solitude. Even thought I was unaware of why any of this was happening, it was during this time that I was introduced to contemplation, meditation, self-reliance, and independence.

  Years later, came to see that my along time had its purpose, and it was to guide me to communed with the soul. It was in contemplating its myriads of light, splendor, and grace that I learned the vastness of my soul.

Rev. Rina A. González

My Parents

*It is only with the heart that one can see rightly;
what is essential is invisible to the eye.*
Antoine De Saint-Exupery

    Both my parents were wonderful human beings who lost their sanity the same way every other parent does, by having children. Both of them had a great sense of humor, although my father was more of a crowd pleaser than my mother ever was. My father was a man for all seasons. He was a dreamer, a self taught musician and a craftsman, whose talents and artistic abilities are a part of everything I think, say, and do. He was a visionary, a teacher and student of life who saw in me what took me years to discover and come to terms with. My mother was a beautiful woman who fell in love with my father at a young age. She loved her children, husband, family, and friends. She was a great cook, made the best homemade desserts ever, who commanded attention from everyone, by saying what was on her mind. While my father gave his children reasons to dream, our mother gave us reason to ponder. Pipo spoiled us, reason why Mima became the disciplinarian in our home.

    My parents were deeply in love, yet never learned the definition of tact. Therefore, quarrels would ensue out of thin air to go back from hence it had come. However, my parents did not know that once energy is dispersed it could not be pulled back. Because of the quarrels, the energy in our home was contaminated and no one knew how to fix things or how to harmonize the environment in the home or in our lives.

    As a holistic healer, who works with energy, see the importance of keeping our bodies and environment clean and free from contaminants. Have often wondered if the contaminated energy in our home, brought about by silly power struggle, did not serve as a conduit to make matters worse for all of us; know it did for me. Remember that my skin would literally rot and because of the condition, I was in constant pain; then again, so were my parents. While what happened in our lives was not done intentionally, what remains true is that our parent's disharmony created devastation for everyone and from this contaminated perception was how we, their children, grew and viewed life.

If there is anything that I am certain of, is that our parents loved us. Today, as I look back, it is obvious that my parents lacked knowing that life could be lived differently. Yet, in the absence of not knowing how to have the life they so deserved, the same scenes, full of illogical choices where played out.

Yes! My parents were clueless about how to live their lives and when my time came to prove them wrong, I too suffered from the same syndrome. Yet, these ill-equipped people were the ones I choose to be my parents. I sometimes wonder if part of being divine is forgetting who we are, as if forgetting, somehow gave us permission to act so foolishly.

Upon my father's death in September of 1958, life changed rather abruptly for the people he loved the most, his wife and five children. Our mother had to assume the role of father and mother and did so willingly. At age 36, she became the breadwinner, something for which she had no prior experience or training. She managed to go from wife, mother, and homemaker, to a versatile and efficient self-reliant woman in every respect. Mima was a warrior, a survivor, and in time, she came to see that she could do anything she set her mind to. Slowly, she stopped being our father's wife to become a full-grown version of herself; an independent woman.

Our mother was the one who gave us the will to live as well as the permission to move on with our lives. She held the light for us in our father's absence and talked about him constantly, to the point that every child in our family knows

Pipo personally and intimately. You can say that she started the tradition of keeping our father's memory alive, which we, their children, have continued doing to this day.

In my estimation, my mother did a remarkable job, yet few saw her valor. The onlookers confused her pain for anger and the peanut gallery repeated what was said, not realizing that words have power, and that this power can either uplift or destroy the individual. I wonder what those who criticized my mother would have done in her predicament. How would they have acted? What would they have done better or different from what she did?

People hide the different aspects of themselves that they do not understand. In my mother's case, being that she was overwhelmed and fearful, she wanted to cover her vulnerability. And by taking on the role of tough, she made herself to be what she was not. I came to know my mother well and know her to be an amazing person. I am a witness to her sleepless nights, to how hard she worked to keep a roof over our heads, food on the table and clothes on our backs. I am grateful for everything she did in our father absence, for I know that in his absence was when she light shined the brightest. She was there when we were growing up, when we got married, when we had children. She was the witness to the person we have become. Our mother knew her children's strengths and weaknesses and knew what our hearts and souls held. Perhaps this is the reason why she made sure that our heads were not full of illusions, so that later, we would not suffer from buyers-remorse. Unfortunately, to many, her way of saying things went against their nature reason why the message got lost in translation. Yet a person's misapprehension does not equal words of wisdom being called by any other name.

Very little compassion was shown to this remarkable woman, reason why today I pay homage to her on behalf of all her children, including myself, as well as on behalf of her grandchildren, great-grandchildren, and great-great-grandchildren.

It is obvious that our mother was not the only one who suffered Pipo's death. I know only too well that we became dysfunctional the very instant that the label 'orphan' reached our tender ears. After our fathers' passing, the little cohesiveness that existed among us disappeared. There was no understanding, no compassion, and many consequences. Life became a free for all, as if each unit pulled the cord of their own discontent to its very limit.

For me, life became difficult in many ways. While I walked, talked, and seemed coherent, something inside of me had died. Not till later, was I able to recuperate part of what was lost. What followed were episodes after episodes of delusional behavior. I got married, to the same man in different body suits, had children, hoping that by some miracle they would be sane, healthy, well-rounded individuals, when I lacked the sanity or clarity of mind that I wanted to give them. As I matured came to terms with the difficulties of my early years as coming to terms with both my parents, I know that they did the best they could with the tools they had. Had they known better I am sure they would have done better.

Yet, who is to say that what happened in our lives did not go according to God's Divine Plan for even though at times I disagreed with their way of reasoning or acting, they did influence me in become the person I am today. Is a matter of fact, the noble idea I had of doing a better job than they had, came to an abrupt halt the day my daughter Silvia was born. As I looked at the baby resting comfortably in my arms, with tears of joy running down my cheeks, saw that what had seemed illogical could be probable. Even went as far as to think, that perhaps my parents had done something right after all.

Rev. Rina A. González

1944, Year of the Wood Monkey

*Hatred never ceases with hatred
but by love alone is it healed.
This is an ancient and eternal law.*

As a soul, I chose Havana Cuba as my birthplace and June 11, 1944 as my birthday. In those days, Cuba had recently earned her independence from Spain with the assistance of her closest neighbor and ally to the North, the USA, in what came to be known as, 'The Maine Incident'.

In 1936, the US came out of its financial depression and in 1941 got involved in <u>WWII</u> after the Pearl Harbor attack on December 7th, of the same year. The world's economy was on a downward spiral. No matter what the individual's social ladder was, everyone suffered the consequences of this terrible war. As a close allied of the USA, Cuba fought along side her neighbor during <u>WWII</u>. You can say that Cuba returned the favor for the USA's earlier intervention and had casualties and losses of her own during this conflict.

In those days, the mood of the world could not have been a happy one. Those in the front line had signed up for a fate yet undetermined. And the ones that stayed behind grew a healthier backbone, which made them resilient, determined, courageous, and more forgiving. As a child, <u>WWII</u> was not in the forefront of my experience, yet this period of our history fascinated me and have read enough to know of its catastrophic effects on the whole of humanity.

I do not believe that any war is a just act as I know that any violence is senseless. The act alone makes us weak, even cynical. Not to mention that any war is an event were no one wins. Even more shocking is the fact that both sides pray to the same god for victory. I marvel at the insanity of individuals who believe that they are just or correct in assuming that God is listening to them and that some how, he has giving them permission to kill another fellowman.

My father's view on any upheaval was very simple. He would have nothing to do with any of it. I remember the day when a friend of the family came to visit my parents in our home in Queens, NY. During the conversation, the young man asked my father for help with his cause. His cause consisted of buying bonds for Cuba's Revolution to overthrow Batista.

My father looked at the friend and said, "Tell me that my money would go to buy two bullets, one for Batista, and one for Castro and I will buy every bond you have." The young man looked at my father and said, "I cannot guarantee that." To what my father replied, "Then I cannot help you. You see, he added, I cannot help a cause that goes against my principals. And looking into the young man's eyes said; of one thing I am certain and it is that the only ones who will suffer the consequences of our actions will be the innocent, and that I will not be a part of."

Years later, my mother witnessed the story's conclusion. My father had passed, Castro had come into power in January of 1959, and the young man had gone back to Cuba only to find that he had been wrong in his decision. Upon realizing the outcome of his choice, he returned to the states a brokenhearted man. During his first visit to my mother, he told her; "Al was right in not having bought bonds from me that day. I am glad that he took no part in the pain that my ignorance has caused."

Rev. Rina A. González

While I do not like wars, know that wars exist because inside each one of us lives the spark of fear and hate that ignites the flame of discord. Until this is understood and at the personal level work on and removed, wars will continue to exist in our lives, in our homes, and in every country of the world.

The Contract of the Soul ~ Revised Edition 2011

As My World Turned

A fresh attitude starts to happen when we look to see that yesterday was yesterday, and now it is gone; today is today and now it is new. It is like that ~ every hour, every minute is changing. If we stop observing change, then we stop seeing everything as new.

Dzigar Kongtrul Rinpoche

In October of 1944, a category 3 hurricane hit Cuba. In those days' preparations for this catastrophic event consisted of using what was around the house for protection.

Our wooden table severed as our barricaded from the winds and water of this hurricane. I will go under the 'assumption' that I was placed in a basket, Flora, my older sister, was given a toy to play with, and the volume was raised on the radio while we still had power, as my parents listen to the weather forecast from underneath Kitchen Central, I mean our bunker, better known as our wooden kitchen table. Under these rudimentary conditions, our family weathered the storm, fortunately, with our lives, home, and sanity intact.

I imagine that my parents, because of their different personalities, one was a worried while the other one was not. My father being the worrier, very possible would have preferred having a rowboat near by, just in case the need arose. While my mother was probably thinking that he was overdoing it and might have even taken a nap. All I know is that what ever happened that day it could not have been too bad because to this day I love windy days, as well as admire the power of lighting and thunder. Do not recall becoming a worrier or aloof because my parents were this way or that way. The reason I say this is that that I know that by nature am aloof, as the next narrative will demonstrate. Years later, living in N.Y., made it to work under one of the worst snow blizzards recorded having only two complaints; {1}- the snow did not let me see where I was going, and {2} - the subways were running slow that day. What I love about New Yorkers is that everyone minds their own business. This day proved to fall under the same category as no one asked me why I was out in such bad conditions and it did not occurred to me to ask what was happening.

I arrived at the office mid morning to find that I was the only one there. The only lights in the office came from the emergency back up system, yet made the best of things. The relaxed atmosphere in the office was soothing and a welcoming change from the hectic pace of a full office. At 24 had been promoted to assistant credit manager in the Loews Credit Department in NYC. Loews was one of the first corporations to give credit cards to their guest and customers. In those days, payments were made by cash or check. All checks that bounced fell under my jurisdiction. Part of my responsibilities was to process the NSF checks, report them to the credit managers, and collected the money owed.

I was young, pretty, sexy, and wet behind the ears and not knowing any better, loved my job. What is even more interesting is how I got the job. It all began the day I went to Loews Human Resource Department, across from CBS Studio's in NYC. A person came out from one of the offices saying that a bi-lingual person {Spanish-English} was needed for the collection department. I stood and said that I spoke both languages. Then remember being given the address, name of the person I was going to see, and the appointment time. Within 45 minutes, I was hired and started to work for Loews the next day.

The Contract of the Soul ~ Revised Edition 2011

This was my first experience as a collector and everything about it was new to me. I was not used to people hanging up on me, yet quickly learned that this was part of what **is** and did not allow the small stuff to upset me. Remember that one by one of my co-workers came over to my cubicle and introduced themselves, and before leaving, wished me luck and handed me their worst cases. Not knowing any better thanked them for their kindness and called each one of the persons on the cards they gave me.

Then a little miracle happened as those that I called paid what they owed. The money rolled into the office and this helped me get noticed right of way, however, how I became Assistant Credit Manager came 8 days later during a call that I will never forget. That day, while making my daily calls came across the longest last name I had ever seen. It had two vowels, the rest were consonants, had no earthly idea how to pronounce it, so without giving it another thought, dialed the number and soon the man's secretary answered. I immediately asked, "Is he in?", and she replied, "one moment Mrs. So, and so". Moments later, a man picked up the extension and said, "Yes, Dear." I introduced myself by saying that while I was not dear I was glad to have him on the phone and explained the nature of my call. This man owed more than $4,000 and God knows why he had not paid. Here I was fresh off the streets speaking to the one customer that every other collector in the Credit Department had tried 'unsuccessfully' to speak with and had failed.

The man started to laugh and said, "you are good and I am paying everything I owe today." Not only that, he added, "I am calling Tisch {Robert Preston Tisch} to let him know about you." As promised, the money was paid and on the 8th day of having started to work for Lowes Hotels as a collector was promoted to the Assistant Credit Manager's position. Even remember having said, - why me? - To my then boss,

Andy Medici, who smiled as he patted me on my back. No one ever believed what happened with the call that started it all. I thank my lucky stars for having been at the right place at the right time and for having such a great outlook on life. If nothing else, my aloofness proved that anything is possible, if you only try. Shortly thereafter, the company started to promote from within. A meeting took place to inform all employees that they could apply for any position within the corporation as they became available. Andy looked straight at me and said, "Rina, the only position that is not available to you, is mine."

<u>Now, back to the blizzard.</u> I was very relaxed and was able to finish the pending work in my IN basket. The silence in the office took me to feel the peace inside me and was grateful that in the middle of the storm I was in a safe place. Felt hunger pains but could not go out because everything was closed in Manhattan, the snow had blocked the doors preventing entering or exiting, yet found plenty of leftovers in the lunchroom and luckily was enough to last me for the two days that I was inside the office. To be perfectly honest the only things I missed, besides my children, was not having a toothbrush and paste in my purse. My winter coat was heavy and furry and it served as a cover during the night.

Around 5:00 o'clock that afternoon, gazed out the window of my office at 1540 Broadway 17th Floor, and was mesmerized by the power of the wind. One thought lead to another and started to compare the rage of the wind to that of human behavior. I laughed at the thought yet continued the game of comparing the two to find that even at her worse moments, Mother Nature is much kinder and gentler that humans can ever be.

Observed how the wind moved the snow from one place to another, as if the she had invisible hands and knew what she was doing. The wind continued the game of picking up the snow and placing it in another pile. Even more amazing was the willingness of the snow not to resist the wind's force. The same snow was being recycled, rejuvenated, and remolded into a different pile while remaining clean and pure.

In the midst of chaos, there was logic, rhythm, and beauty in Mother Nature's movement; so much so, that I became aware that I was witnessing grace at work. It was in contemplating the force of the wind that I understood that humanity has two sources; Spirit and Nature.

Intuitively knew that humanity's disharmonies come from not knowing our strength and perfection. Father God is our spirit nature, Mother God is our human nature. After all, who can disagree that we are souls having a physical experience or that we have Mother Nature's minerals, proteins, and chemical compounds inside of us? Then, why I wondered, coming from such beauty, power and grace do humans create disharmonies, when all we have to do is go with the flow of life, and from our center of glory use our spiritual gifts to weather life's storms?

Rev. Rina A. González

References

1. ***The Maine Incident*** ~ The Cuban struggle for independence had captured the American imagination for years, and newspapers had been agitating for intervention with sensational stories of Spanish atrocities against the native Cuban population, intentionally sensationalized and exaggerated. This continued even after Spain replaced Weyler and changed its policies and American public opinion was very much in favor of intervening in favor of the Cubans. In January 1898, a riot by Cuban Spanish loyalists against the new autonomous government broke out in Havana, leading to the destruction of the printing presses of four local newspapers for publishing articles critical of Spanish Army atrocities. The US Consul-General cabled Washington with fears for the lives of Americans living in Havana. In response, the battleship **USS *Maine*** was sent to **Havana** in the last week of January. On February 15, 1898, the Maine was rocked by an explosion, killing 268 of the crew and sinking the ship in the harbor. The cause of the explosion has not been clearly established to this day. In an attempt to appease the US, the colonial government took two steps that had been demanded by President **William McKinley**: it ended forced relocation from homes and offered negotiations with the independence fighters. But the truce was rejected by the rebels.

2. ***Between mid-1942 until early 1944....*** Seven Cuban ships were sank by German submarines (U-Boat) in actions where were killed more than eighty Cuban marines and three

Americans. These ships were torpedoed and cannonaded by the ships from Germany that were marauding, acting as spies, on our territorial waters. As an evocation of these fatal encounters there are at least two monuments erected to the fallen Cuban sailors. One of these is located at Avenida del Puerto and O'Reilley Street, on an obelisk in front of the sea in the municipality Habana Vieja and the other one is in the city of Cienfuegos, in the park The Mambí, which is opposite to the Recreation Center Los Pinitos. This monument was built thanks to the contribution of the residents of queen neighborhood, to leave a memory of the victim's sailors aboard the ship Mambí. Finally, in the maritime theme of war, says the book "Following the German mark in Cuba", that a Cuban flag hunting submarine (CS - 13) on May 15th 1943 was able to overturn the German spy submarine at the southeast of the lighthouse, located in Cayo Bahia de Cadiz, near Nuevitas. Continuing the theme of the Cuban-German relation during World War II, in the book we read that once the war was declared to Japan, Italy and Germany in our country were created internment camps, also called the enemy's concentration camps or prisons in the municipality of Arroyo Arenas for women and others for men in Tiscornia, Torrens and Isle of Pines. In 1941 arrived to Cuba, the German Spy August Kunning Heinz, who using the false name of Henry Augustus Lunin and taking advantage of his knowledge of telegraphy and radio engineering, under the guise of a small trader of Latin American origin, gathered important information and data from diverse nature of sugar, coffee, and tobacco productions in Cuba. Also, the German spy informed to the intelligence German corpse about the tonnage, capacity, and nautical possibilities of the Cuban maritime fleet, which made its voyages between Cuban ports and host ports in Europe, U.S. and other countries of

Southern American Continent. These reports allowed the actions of sinking Cuban ships in Manzanillo and Santiago de Cuba, in 1942, as is quoted above. He was discovered by the Cuban intelligence forces who found maps, sketches and drawings of Cuban malls and different communication equipment both recipients and long-range transmitters and demonstrative documents of his contacts with other Nazis, and a curious pen-gun, that is, at present, exhibited in the Museum and Public Library Oscar Maria de Rojas, in Cardenas, Matanzas. This curious firearm taken from the Nazi spy, measures 14.5 centimeters long and 2.5 wide and it was manufactured in the United States, because presented engraved an inscription: The Lake Erie Chemical Co., Cleveland Ohio, USA. Of 12 mm caliber, with a single shot and a trigger in button form, this lethal weapon called Pocket Pistol or Pencil Gun, which was fashionable in the late 19th century and the first four decades of the 20th century. It was used mainly by travelers, players, professionals, light women, and spies in many countries of the world. *By: Raul Martell – Source: Cubarte, Portal of Cuban Culture.*

3. ***Hurricane of October 1944 Cuba-Florida:***

The 1944 Cuba–Florida hurricane (also known as the Pinar del Río Hurricane of 1944 and 1944 Havana Hurricane) was a large, intense Category 3 hurricane that affected western Cuba and Florida. The eleventh tropical cyclone, seventh hurricane, and third major hurricane of the season developed over the southern Caribbean Sea on October 12. It intensified to a hurricane on October 13, attained its peak on October 17, and struck Pinar del Río with gusts in excess of 160 mph (260 km/h). The hurricane accelerated, and it struck southwest Florida near Sarasota on October 19. It diminished to a tropical storm, briefly exited over water off southeast Georgia, and moved inland near Savannah on October 20. It became extra tropical over southeastern Virginia on October 21. The late-season October storm was eventually responsible for very heavy rains, a wide swath of destruction, and over 300 deaths, especially in rural areas of Cuba.

4. ***The Blizzard of 1969 ~ February 8-10, 1969*** ~ Write up found from an Ancestor.com Community written by Dave Tuttle ~ Known as the "Lindsay Storm", this blizzard paralyzed the metropolitan areas of New York and Boston for three days, from February 8th to February 10th, 1969. The storm consisted of two areas of low pressure. One in the Ohio Valley, which had weakened after moving through the Rockies, while the other one was forming off the coast of Virginia. This secondary low-pressure area intensified rapidly and moved up the east coast to Cape Cod. The heaviest snow fell in a band from the New York City area to the White Mountains in New Hampshire. Both New York and Boston received their fair share of snow with over 20 inches apiece. My own experience of this storm was a series of singular events. Just two weeks into a new full-time job at IBM in Cambridge, Mass., I had flown down to LaGuardia Airport on the Eastern air shuttle, visiting for the weekend at my parents' home in Pelham Manor, New York. When the storm descended on the area, getting back to Boston was something of an adventure... The airports were closed, of course, so I decided to take the train. Pelham is the last train station outside of the city, just 31 minutes from Grand Central Station in Manhattan.

A brave taxi cab driver took me to the Pelham station, swimming through 8 inches or more of snow on the ground with more coming down heavily. I caught the train into the city, heading for the express train from Grand Central to Boston's South Station. In New York, I waited in line for my ticket to Boston; the station was busy but not jammed. By chance I overheard the person behind me in line was also going to Boston, but he was turned away -- the train was full, and I had gotten the last ticket! I found out later that my train inbound was the last train that came into Grand Central that day, and the train to Boston was the last train that left -- the station was closed by the storm, an almost unheard-of event. The storm pounded the Northeast. Bedford, Massachusetts recorded 25 inches of snow, New York City had 20 inches, and Portland, Maine ended up with 22 inches. The storm got its nickname from John Lindsay, the Mayor of New York City at the time. His poor handling of the events before, during, and after the storm made many New Yorkers angry with him, and it all but devastated his re-election chances. His snow removal crews were slow to respond because of inaccurate weather forecasts, and sections of New York City remained unplowed for a week after the storm. On the train to Boston, we all felt a bit lucky; no other transportation was moving. At first, I could not find a seat, but outrageous coincidence played its hand again -- in the next car I ran into Fred Abramson and his fiancée. Fred and I were college roommates in the spring of 1967, and I had shared an off-campus apartment with him that summer. The three of us talked and shared snacks and took turns sitting and standing as the unexpected hours went by. The train stopped twice for an hour or more between New York City and New Haven to let the railroad plows clear the track ahead of us. What was normally a 4- to 5-hour trip stretched into 9 1/2 hours -- an overnight adventure ride through a major blizzard, but we made it! We arrived about 6:30 in the morning at Boston's Back Bay Station, greeted by clearing skies and bright sunshine and almost two feet of snow on the ground. By chance, I had gotten the last train into New York, then the last ticket on the last train to leave!

5. ***Preston Robert "Bob" Tisch*** (April 29, 1926–November 15, 2005) was the chairman, and, with his brother Laurence, part owner of the Loews Corporation. Tisch was born in the Bensonhurst section of Brooklyn in 1926. On August 16, 1986, he was appointed Postmaster General of the United States Postal Service, serving until February 1988. Tisch received a BA degree in economics from the University of Michigan in 1948, and his wife Joan Tisch and his daughter received degrees at the university. While in college, Tisch was a member of Sigma Alpha Mu, a Jewish fraternity. From 1991 until his death, Tisch owned 50 percent of the New York Giants American football team. Tisch died in 2005 in his Manhattan home after a yearlong battle with an inoperable brain tumor.

The Contract of the Soul ~ Revised Edition 2011

The Visit

"Do not waste precious energy in small stuff; instead, focus your unlimited potential on what you want to manifest knowing that all your needs will be met."

Rev. Rina

    I remember the day when my I Am Presence, [my Guardian Angel], came to visit. Our eyes met as memories of our adventures came to life. A deep sense of gratitude came over me for having experienced life so many times under his guidance, and although knew that I had made progress, there was more work that needed to be done.

    We smiled as the colors of purple, red, and orange created a tapestry of artwork in the evening skies. What a magnificent view! It seemed that God handpicked these colors to show us how love was created. In that moment the energy of love was all around us. We smiled, laughed as more memories came into view. We flew among the colors and glided close to the stars, and there, among this panoramic view was Planet Earth in her rotation among the other planets. She looked harmonious without a care . Perhaps her harmony comes from knowing how much she is loved and how much she is needed in the Cosmos, as she is needed and loved by every soul that is born under her tutelage.

    If humans could see what I was witnessing, perhaps they too would be at peace with life and with themselves. The view of earth from on high is breath taking and the higher I flew she became a dot at a distance, until she turned into a speck of dust that glittered in the night. All of the sudden realized that I was flying by myself and that my Guardian Angel was way below me, gesturing me to come down. Started my descend asking myself why he had come to visit and it was then that I realized that the reason why I had soared was in the hopes that he would be gone by the time I got back.

Once back, sat and talked for hours. Our conversation was about life's basic needs as well as death, rebirth, and the ambiguity in which humanity finds itself in, which comes directly from not knowing its' purpose or role in life. "Life was never supposed to be anything but an opportunity to learn, said he, yet the opposite occurs when the message is misunderstood." How can a message of light, faith, and hope be conveyed, when there are so few willing to listen? - asked I, not realizing that now he had my attention.

For those, who are not familiar with the Guardian Angel Work Manual, its function or how it works, allow me to give you a quick overview. What every person wants more than anything else is to be whole, to be complete. As well, know that the only one with the power and authority to complete us is our individualized I Am Presence or Guardian Angel.

Humans, have heard that we have a Guardian Angel, yet few have tried contacting their source. While speaking of angels is common practice, what few humans have done is understand what they hear. Speaking without having the correct information is the same as speaking half-truth's and when our greatest asset is not understood, while the presence never diminishes the contact cannot become as strong as it should.

Humans long to have closeness in their lives. The longing we feel is for our other half, as glimpses of our closeness are remembered. Yet not knowing this, our longing is taking to mean that we are falling in love. Unfortunately, ignoring our deepest truth, longing for our Higher Self is interpreted as the human need to mate. Reason why falling in love happens as frequently as falling out of love, and our

Higher Self or Guardian Angel is given many names, such as but not limited to:

- Our Split Apart
- Our Soul Mate
- And The Love of Our Life

    The list goes on, and depending on what part of the world you are from or live in, our greatest strength is called by different names, reason why we keep on searching for what we are missing in the opposite sex, when what we are searching for is already ours and is within our reach.

    Our Individualized Guardian Angel and our soul, are part of the same Divine Spark that emerged from the whole of creation eons ago. Even though the spark split into two separate and equal parts, they have remained united sharing the same essence throughout eternity. One forms the I Am Presence, who is, approximately 15' above your crown chakra. The other half of the same spark of divinity is your soul, situated at the second chakra of your spine known as the Sex Chakra, or Seat-of-the-Soul Chakra. The connection to our Guardian Angel comes through the Crown Chakra. This connection is pure energy. Said energy travels down the spine touching and awaking the spiritual memories that are stored inside the cells of the body.

    Our Guardian Angel's job is to guide and protect us through life as well as remind us to learn our lessons. He is the record keeper and when you want to know something, who better than him to give you the answers you seek? "What God has joined together let no man put asunder"; this is the bond that no man can break, this is the tie that binds. Sadly, the union between our Higher Self and our Divinity has been misunderstood for eons, and when something as noble and as important as this is, misunderstood, everything else falls under the same category ~ "confusion."

As a result, confusion is the state of mind in which humanity finds itself in and unless this paradigm is changed, confusion will remain undefeated, unchallenged, and unstoppable. Our Guardian Angel is our truest essence, our highest truth, from where a deeper meaning of life emerges. Find your source, connect to it, use this power wisely and you will never be alone again.

Before souls reincarnate they undergo a learning process. Apparently, I missed the course of *Guardian - Angel Awareness 101,* which is essential to having a good working relationship with my source and because of my aloofness, my Guardian Angel had a lot of nudging to do in order to get my attention. Especially when I did not want to be bothered with, the minutia of learning or coming to terms with the fact that I was alive and had to work to do.

To me life is simple, and if I do what comes naturally the lesson is learned yet I was missing a part of the lesson because for years had be told, that I might be the cause of something that thought I was trying to prevent. No matter how imperfect I was or still am, there is one thing of which I am certain, I have been here many times before. This time, my goal is to get this living thing right making this my final trip. You see I miss my place far far away in the land beyond the region of thunder, in a land that is always peaceful, always serene, and bright with the resplendent glory of God as my constant companion.

Since I am a human being, one that has made countless mistakes, chose to bypass the small stuff in life eliminating the confusion and delays to which I am so familiar with. Feel that the work done thus far is a good start, but know that if left undone, this incarnation would again prove that Pete and Repeat are alive, and well.

The Contract of the Soul ~ Revised Edition 2011

The Invitation

In joy and sorrow all things are equal, be guardian of all, as of yourself.

Shantideva

    As we were saying, here I was enjoying my home in a place far far away, when my Guardian Angel came to visit. Even though I was pleased to see him, wondered why he had come and as I tried to be a good hostess missed the crescent moon's extravaganza at daybreak.

    His words of wisdom poured from his lips as I listened to every syllable knowing that he was right. "You see, - he said, man gets caught up in living his life and forgets how powerful he truly. And by forgetting his brilliance is why man becomes vulnerable." Then again, how can man remember his brilliance when he is disassociated from his spiritual powers – asked I? He smiled in agreement, as we both stood and walked around the terrace, I watering the plants as he looked at me. Yet, my thoughts were not on the watering of the plants but on the fact that he was still there, right next to me. As I looked up saw daybreak approaching and it was then that I realized the seriousness of his visit.

    I had just retuned, however his presence indicated that I was going back. When is he leaving – I wondered, as the plants got soaked. It was then that I saw glimpses of my last incarnation. An immense feeling of joy came over me as memories of the work done came to mind. Felt good knowing that I had contributed to the empowerment of women, yet had not anticipated becoming passionate about the cause. Smiled in seeing how simple life is when it is seen through the eyes of the all knowing 'hindsight' and how every struggles that man encounters comes from lacking rhythm in his movement through life. Said rhythm is present when one fallows their true passion in life.

Here I was hesitant about going back, when in truth I was, negating feeling the joy that following true passing gives. To me life is a treasure trove filled with numerous probabilities. Not to mention that what I love doing is exploring, learning, evolving, growing, helping, and teaching. Sat next to him knowing that the time had come, and that I could either be a willing participant of the experience or prolong the agony by joining him kicking and screaming, which I had already done and proved to be no fun for either one.

My mind was going faster and faster; as one thought ended, another one began, and it was then that I realized that he had read every one of my thoughts. He smiled and said, "Life can be an enjoyable experience. You already have all that you will ever need to be triumphant in everything you do. Just remember to be true to who you are and do what comes naturally."

He walked over to the railing and staring into my eyes said, "In time, everything will become clear to you. What you do not understand today will one day be part of your awareness. Your job is to learn and to be obedient to spirit's call. My job is to give you the desire *'to live again'* so that what started eons ago can come full circle as our victory is recorded in the annals of time for a job well done. Remember that everything you learn is to be shared and whatever you chose to experience is how your life will be. Make sure that your life is full of wondrous, unforgettable moments, for this will take you to experience more of the same."

Dawn was upon us and rain had started to fall. We walked inside hand in hand and it was then that our eyes met again, as he asked, "Would you live again?" Saw his penetrating blue eyes smiling at me and could only say; "I don't like pain." He smiled and holding me tightly said, "Live above confusion." We both laughed, embraced, becoming a single light that disappeared at first light. We traveled in the light for several minutes and knew that we were close to earth for even though there were clouds around us, the sun was farther away.

And as we approached earth's gravitational pull had this thought. "Life is a game, a game that has rules. Life's rules are understood as you play the game of life. It matters not if you win or lose the game, for as you play the game it is that life is lived. I am going on a new adventure, so I might as well play the game of life with zest." Have to say, that to the present day, that is exactly what I have done.

Rev. Rina A. González

The Contract of the Soul ~ Revised Edition 2011

This Thing Called Life!

What's this that runs through me?
Is like a power that makes me be.
Could this be life or is this heaven?
Is there such thing as being free?

I have heard say that life is an illusion
That takes us up and down as in a game.
Yet know that my soul while is an essence
Enjoys lives experiences and glee.

Did I come back to live or be bewildered?
Or could it be that echoes are just sounds
Which comes from lives not yet determined,
Or, is the past we've lived the echoing sound?

I get confused when I think of such delusions,
Yet this is what has bound me to life's sounds.
To me, life is entertaining yet elusive
I want to find the answers of her might.

Thus far, I have come to see the wonders
That this thing called life offers the soul.
Yet no matter how much it entertains me
A part of me that still will not budge.

While the mind wants me to denounce it,
The soul proclaimed its goodness from the start.
So I guess that if life is real in the nighttime,
Then life has to be real in the morn.

The Contract of the Soul ~ Revised Edition 2011

Accepting the Invitation

*"I came into the world to comfort those who need comforting,
And to create discomfort for those who are too comfortable"...*

Never knew that an invitation could be so painful. Yet here I was going through the birth canal, and both, my mother and I were in pain. In a flash, went from being warm to cold, from silence to noise, from darkness to light. I went from comfortable, to feeling that I was in the air wobbling and crying, to find that some idiot had me hanging from my feet as he spanked my bottom. What an entrance! All this so oxygen would enter my lungs. This is how I took my first breath, sobbing and crying uncontrollably. The thing is that I was already alive before the 'doctor' hit me. So, why spank a child for the child to do what the child will do naturally? Without a doubt, birth was my first trauma!

Was I welcome into the world? Was I thanked for having chosen my parents to guide and protect me in this incarnation? No! I, like so many others who come to Planet Earth was not welcomed or thanked for having joined the sea of humanity. Can you imagine the quality of life this would have provided millions of us? The mere recognition of the soul would have brought harmony to all life form on the planet. If you are among the millions who were not welcomed or thanked at time of birth, you have the right to do so right now by following these simple steps.

- Looking east call Mother Gaia {Earth's Guardian Angel} and ask her to welcome you to her planet.

- Tell Mother Gaia that you are willing to learn your lessons but that from this moment forward

you want to learn them in joy, love, light, health, compassion, abundant and prosperity.
- Then thank yourself for having come to experience life and live your life fully.

You can do this ritual for yourself and for any of your children that are under 14 years of age. If the child is over 14, then the individual has to do the ritual for him or her self. According to tribal customs, 14 is the age when rights to rituals are gained, of which this is one of many. Following these simple steps will bring a shift in consciousness and you will notice life becoming lighter, easier to understand and manage. When you become aware that a shift in consciousness has occurred, seat and ponder on what has taken place. Smile and thank *Mother Gaia* again, and thank her every time she comes into your mind, which will be often.

Now, let us go back to my birth: In recalling the day's events, trying to make sense of what had happened, while was able to see glimpses of my conversation with my Guardian Angel, was unsure how I had gotten here and somehow felt that I had missed something, yet could not put my finger on what '**it**' was. Therefore, to date, what happened between our last words and my birth remains a mystery. Maybe I do not want to remember how a spark of divinity went from having it all to being crammed in a moist place. Or how my legs were rendered useless, to the point of not been able to use them properly for the first few months of my new life. Not to mention that my silly arguments did not work for every attempt to stay behind had failed.

Yes! I was alive, again, and witnessed my birth, its pain and even remember coming down the birth canal. The reason that I finally came out was that something got my attention. While I could not see what it was, know that it was a shiny object. Saw a tunnel followed the sounds and a bright light coming from it. The sounds seemed to be calling out to me to join them in whatever it was that they were doing. The light was so bright that it mesmerized me.

As it turns out the sounds came from the conversation that the nurses and doctor were having trying to figure out why I did not come out. And the light seemed to have vanished the moment I was born. Wait a minute; how can that be? Am I not the light that was born? Can you image that? As humans, we see a bright light when we come into the world and we see it again as we leave. Could it be that we are that bright light that mesmerizes us? I am sure that we are, except not knowing our truth has served only to confuse us, for in accepting the notion that we are imperfect beings, we have kept out own grace out of reach. If I am correct, this is humanities first misconception.

To add insult to injury, I do not remember signing my soul contract, which in no way proves that I did not. To save face I took this as a sign of bravado on my part and decided that from that moment on I would pace myself, which proved to be impossible, because my life was about putting out fires; fires created by my own confusion.

Here I was facing another one of the thing I did not want to experience; rebirth, only because this implied responsibility. I did not want to be responsible for anything or anyone, not ever myself. Kept thinking that I could have stayed in my place, far, far away, yet here I was in another one of my wild goose chases, only this time I landed headfirst. What an adventure. Something else was bothering me. My Guardian Angel said that I did not have to experience pain. Then why was I feeling pain from the unset? Maybe part of learning how to live is going through pain so that you learn to live without it. Something else was troubling me. Do not remember having given an answer, so I guess that not answering is the same as accepting the invitation.

For what its worth, since early on felt that I did not belong; did not like some of my extended family members on my mother's side. Every time they came to visit, which was often, would look towards the sky and ask - Why, God Why? Yet somewhere, somehow, found the importance of being alive as that of being truthful; so I was, am and will always be truthful. See that liars need to have a good memory while a truthful person needs nothing more than his or her words to live by.

However, my truthfulness brought me a difference response that I had anticipated as well as proving that being truthful was important only to me. It was heartbreaking to see the difference between what people say, and what people do. And understand that no one likes being under constant scrutiny. Funny thing, people who lie, don't know that they lie, yet they keep lying. So I was more than happy to point this small detail to the liars in the family and my persistence lead to encounters from those with opposing views. Those that opposed my truth saw me as different from them and wanted me to acclimate to their lies or else. As you can imagine I choose <u>'or else'</u>.

As I look back, see that had I been different, or had those that opposed me been as clear, purposeful, or as sincere as I, maybe no misunderstandings would have taken place. Yet, I am thankful for having had such wonderful teachers pressing hard on my conscious, for indeed they were the fuel that propelled me to become who I am today.

Kept asking spirit why I was here, wanted to know if there was logic to the madness. One day my question was answered with a resounding echo that said; you are here to help! That blew my mind. I could not understand why if I was here to help I was not able to help the liars; God knows I tried. Oh, well maybe they were just supposed to show me to be different. Later came to understand that what I had to learn was to stay away from the little minds that accepted lies as truth.

Ever since that day I have been the voice of clarity and reasoning and while it has taken longer that I would have liked see that my truth is finally making a dent on what is not real. I as so many of you worked for a living. Yes, I had a 'j.o.b'. Actually, I had several and disliked each one. Yet, because of social conditioning, found myself doing what brought me no satisfaction, which is another form of limitation and pain. So what did I do to stop the pain? My solution to the problem was to change jobs, reason why I had so many. While I made good money was unhappy because the job did not fulfill me at the soul level. This changed the day I understood that life is about following your passion and knew that I was not passionate about working for anyone else. However, I did not know how to break my addiction to working nor did I know what else to do in order to bring a paycheck home.

It was then that I discovered that my need to work came from wanting to have 'stuff'. While I had to work to keep a roof over my head, a car for transportation, life, health, car insurance, clothes, shoes, food, recreation, etc., noticed that more money went to buying unnecessary stuff; stuff that brought me discomfort instead of peace. Having these unnecessary stuff brought no comfort to my soul, is a matter of fact, having so much of anything did not make me happy either. It can be said that I was sick and tired of how complicated my life had become, yet did not know how to keep a roof over my head or put food on the table without having to resort to the old habit of working for a living.

The day came when I finally understood that I had fallen prey to the 'Pete and Repeat' syndrome of the ages. As you can image, was not too happy to see that out of ignorance had conformed to doing what I so disliked. As fast as possible, set out to free myself from the wheel of demand and supply, knowing that I had gotten myself into the cycle and knew that I would find the way to get out. Except had not anticipated that demand is ever-present, and supply comes at a price.

Felt terrible in seeing how I had betrayed myself. Saw how I had fallen victims to social conditioning. It was then that I swore that once I learned how to become free I would teach others so that they too could be free. Started to write down everything I bought and at the end of the month added the money that I had wasted on stuff. I can tell you countless stories of the things that ended in the trash, or were given to charity, or sat idle as dust collectors in my house. This needed to stop. Day by day, I worked on seeing why and how I had become addicted to having things and it was then that I was able to see that my need to shop was an urge. Soon thereafter, saw that a shopaholic is fueled by the same urge than a drug or alcohol addict is. All addictions are euphoric in nature, as the need to shop or to use drug or drink alcohol comes from the same place and they are all co-dependencies or flaws of the personality.

From then on anytime I went shopping filling the cart with the useless stuff that I was used to buying, except before getting on line to pay I asked myself; Do you really need these things? Inevitably the answer was NO. Then I would walk back to the place from where I had gotten the item and placed it back. After a few times of this exercise in futility I no longer felt the needed to continue going shopping for unnecessary stuff. All humans come into the world with spiritual gifts and one of my gifts involves audio sensory, which in my line of work is used to listen, receive, and discern messages. The train ear hears spirit's voice, while the untrained ear thinks that what it hears is something else. That whispers in your ear is the answer to a question that you mentally asked a few moments before. Be smart and start listening to spirit's voice and you will be surprise as the difference this will make in your life. Among the things that I had heard, one was very distinctive. The message said; "Do what's in your nature." Fortunately, after years of ignoring the message I finally came to understand that I could make a living doing what is in my nature. Have to confess that I have never been happier nor have I ever had the need to look back. While letting go of my old ways was not easy, have to say that having the courage to change has brought me the peace I so desired.

Do whatever you need to do in order to change those things in your life that are harmful or non-productive. If in order to obtain what you want out of life you need to go without, then go without. In the end, you will find that life has a deeper meaning once you let go of what is making you sick and tired of being sick and tired. Today I no longer have the need to own anything that has the power to keep me in shackles. Through it all, see this period in my life as an opportunity of experiencing how it feels to go after a dream and of making my dream a reality. I also know that because of my determination was that life changed. I am grateful that I no longer feel the need to comply with what is habitual in nature or conform to what social conditioning dictates. What is even more interesting is that the money I make doing what I love doing is enough to meet my necessities something that I could never do when I had a 'j.o.b'.

Life changed when I stopped being afraid of the "ifs" in life. It was in following the beat of my heart that the message of yesterday sounded louder that ever before, and in, "Doing what's in my nature" became my way of life. That day there were two roads before me. While one was very familiar to me, the other road, waited to be explored. My choice is obvious. What will yours be?

The Contract of the Soul ~ Revised Edition 2011

"Do what's in your nature!"
Simple Grace

Of all the memories that I hold dear
There is the one of you standing beside me
Holding my hand as you lead the way,
Through the ups and downs of a crazy day.

Have to admit that you made life easy
Guiding me to live each moment as a new beginning,
So that I could find my way and learn why
I had come back to love with a human heart.

Even in those moments when I could not see
How things would turn out, your smile reminded me
That it was all a dream from which I would awake,
To find your wonderful smile lighting the way.

My soul grows the fonder as it realizes
That it hungered only to be by your side.
As I look and find the message within
That with tender care you gave me to keep.

"I've planted the seed that will bring you fruits
So that peace and love are always with you.
And as you awake from the sleeping state
Find meaning to life in a different way.
As your Guardian Angel
Have selected what needs to learned
To clear the path of unconscious deeds.
These things you must do,
If heavenly bound you inspired to".

Rev. Rina A. González

You have shown me how to be pure of heart
By keeping my thoughts clear of any confusion.
Have allowed my spirit to soar to new heights,
And have found dimensions that are deep inside.

As I look in splendor to all that I am
There is a trail of gratitude pressing behind.
From the moment of birth, to the here and now
You have been beside me holding the light.

Maybe only dreamers can understand
The power created by a child's trust,
When at the age of eight I gave you my word
Of being kind to life, and always true to you.

As I sat and talked to you long ago
Knew that your guidance would have from above.
Today as I look at my life can see
Your tender embrace alive within me.

You've loved me, listened, and cared.
You knew I would do the things I came here to do.
But just to make sure you send me earth angels
So that all my dreams would finally come true.

Tell me one thing more; the day I am gone,
When I awake from the sleeping state,
Will I remember that I was alive,
Or only know that I am Sublime?

With your loving eyes looking at me
It would be difficult to remember not
That you were there from the get go,
Through the ups and downs of a crazy day
That your love transformed into *Simple Grace*.

There is comfort in knowing that you lead the way,
My job was made easy; it is to obey.
The command kept saying,
"Do what's in your nature."

And to my amazement,
Found that my true nature is to love all things.
I come from your essence that is clear to see.
So, if I come from your nature, your nature is in me!

Rev. Rina A. González

Awakening!

Spiral may undulate, spiral may rise, or spiral may fall.
But ultimately, the light within you must answer the call.

Guatama Buddha

Discernment and reasoning brings illumination. Action is the root of the verb 'to be'. "Genius is 1% inspiration and 99% perspiration". For life to be a favorable experience, you have to work at it. Every thought, word, and deed, conscious or unconscious, become part of your daily experience. With time, the experience will be stored in the sub-conscious and it is from here that human life will be favorable or unfavorable.

EVERY CONSCIOUS ACT brings good results, while AN UNCONSCIOUS ACT brings unwanted results. Conscious thoughts, words, and deeds bring the results you want to have, while unconsciousness bring what no one wants to experience, yet both come from the same place, the individual's state of mind. It would be prudent to pay attention to the underlying energy that propels any action. Learning how to do things right takes time so be kind to yourself and slow your pace thus avoiding falling into the same old habits or routines.

Learn to readjust to your new way of thinking by taking baby steps. Adjusting to the new process that you are learning and being consciously present in your life is how mistakes are avoided. Rushing through life brings confusion as well as missing the essence of life itself. Be the witness to what you think, say, and do, knowing that good results are guarantied.

Consciousness will prove to be a great allied in your new life. Learning to work with your spiritual powers is very important, as is coming to understand that without your energy, your attention, your command, and your will, 'no thing' that is unconscious" will ever become a manifestation in your life ever again. Look for the underlying energy that creates the same unwanted results, this is how you will prevent them from reoccurring. Coming to understand the process and acclimating to your new life takes time. Change is not difficult yet seldom is change welcomed.

Habits, we will always have, after all, repetition is part of nature. However, what we need to learn is how to make better choices in doing what we do, so that our experiences reflect the perfection of the soul and not the flaws of a mind ruled by ego. As everything else, change comes when you seek it. Unless you are actively looking for ways to improve your life, the only thing that can come your way are the same *unconscious stuff* that by habit you created. Ever heard, "trash in, trash out"? Unfortunately, life is no different.

If your life is not everything you want it can be, then the stuff that you have in your life is impeding you from having the life that you are deserving of. Realize that you are the common denominator in all your relationships and that you need to be in control of your life. You are the link to all past, present and future conditions that you have and will ever experience. Everything, inside and outside of you is a direct reflection of your state of mind.

Everything starts with a thought as is true that your heart holds the key to resolving every situation that arises. Take the time to work on yourself, and before long, you will be on your way to giving birth to a new creation, a brand-new you! Awakening to your new life can be compared to Michelangelo di Lodovico Buonarroti Simoni's work. Think of this man's passion and commitment to excellence who for years carved a piece of marble producing masterpiece after masterpiece, claiming that all he did was chisel the marble to reveal what was already inside the stone. He was also a painter, an architect, a poet and an engineer. The Sistine Chapel was one of his most revered works and the David and the Rome Pieta were two of the world's most treasured sculptures. What this man did so long ago was nothing short of remarkable. Today, the beauty and love of his work can still be felt. Now is time for you to carve a masterpiece and like Michelangelo before you, carve a freer, happier, version of yourself.

Working on yourself is a process that brings higher awareness to all that you think, say, and do, something that to date you have not experienced. As you awaken, your senses will become clearer, sharper, and more alert. Clarity of mind will lead to noticing the 'things' that you have not noticed before. The 'things' that add zest to life will be very real to you. Things like finding life interesting, funny, cute, intriguing, and adventurous. When everything in your life become new, revisit those places that although are familiar to you, were not enjoyed the first time you went there. Learn to appreciate life's beauty by getting to know her intimately and personally!

Do not force yourself by thinking that your goals need to be big, for doing so will only create mental stress and soon will stop doing the required work. Instead, do the task for the sake of the task itself, enjoy the process by assimilating the lesson, the teacher, its beauty, and grace. Feel your body; allow your feelings to guide you. Listen to what your body has to say; hear the body's language. Every part of our body has divine intelligence and each body parts has the capacity to be made a new with time and persistence. The body stores the memories of all experiences. Lodged within the cells are the results of all unconsciousness and conscious deeds.

If your health is not to your satisfaction, take the time to heal its imperfections by replacing fear with love, darkness with light, sadness with joy, illness with health, scarcity with abundance and ignorance with wisdom. Disease is lack of ease and every sickness or disease comes from contaminated energy in your aura and chakras. You should consult a Holistic Healer to ascertain the cause of the illness so that the energy blockages can be removed and your health can recuperate faster.

Place your attention on what you are doing. Do not multitask. Multitasking is a misnomer; our brain can only do one thing at a time and if you are not present in your life, neither is God. While some think that multitasking denotes intelligence, it is in rushing through life that life's wonders are missed. Life is made of small moments, which take place in the present. Moreover, this precious moment will not wait for you, nor will it ever come back. Think of how many precious moments you have missed and then consider that yesterday is gone, tomorrow has not arrived and today is the present; reason why it's a gift.

Ask for guidance and meditate daily. Visit your sanctuary {heart center} as often as possible and learn to notice the many blessings that are already part of your life. Take time to breathe and breathe correctly. If you do not know how to breathe correctly, then learn how to do so. Start giving your body the oxygen, it needs to live a healthy, rewarding, and meaningful life.

You might want to take Yoga classes or perhaps join a meditation group. Do activities that will enhance and benefit your breathing, this will lead to a better life style and a healthier mind set.

The following is a breathing technique that I have used for years.

- Focus on the tip of the nose, slowly inhale on the count of six [6] through both nostrils.

- Hold your breath on the count of three [3].
- Exhale slowly through lips partly open on the count of six [6], placing your attention on the navel.
- Wait to inhale again on to the count of three [3].
- Repeat the process for 10 minutes, for best 15 minutes.

Breathing is the first thing a child does at birth and it will be the last thing a person will do when he or she dies. So breathe often. Fill your life with joy by being the joy you want to have. Bless others and you will be blessed. Be a constant source of laughter and inspiration for those around you and you will never go without. Smile! Go for walks around your neighborhood. Get to know those that are 16 miles around you. They influence your life as you influence theirs.

Go to a park, a lake, or the seashore and witness the miracle of creation taking place before your very eyes. Be grateful for having come this far and for being alive. Know that love is forever present in your heart, mind, and soul, because you come from love. Make love the only energy you have to give and start counting the many blessings that will appear in your life!

The Contract of the Soul ~ Revised Edition 2011

Gratitude

An inner sense of peace comes from a heart filled with love & gratitude!

Rev. Rina

  Count your blessings each day and be grateful to everything that you have in your life. Learn to be grateful for all the good and for all choices made. Failing to see life for what life <u>is,</u> is the same as not seeing life at all. Be grateful for having had the courage to see the truth about your present condition and for the conviction to change your life. Be grateful for every answered prayer, as well as for the unanswered ones. Be grateful for all the souls you've met. Be generous towards life so that life is generous in return.

  When a situation arises with no solution in sight, shed light on it by going towards it in gratitude and love. Light changes and transmutes any obstruction. Gratitude equalizes and love heals. Once you implement these easy to follow steps in your everyday life, you will notice that all unwanted situation eases and in time, vanishes.

  Be grateful for catching yourself repeating the same old habits. Do not get upset, just be mindful that you are a work in progress and that soon the old habits will be replaced with the ones that you are implementing. When you become grateful for all that <u>is,</u> you will see life taking a new meaning and this new awareness will set you on a new path. Be grateful for being the silent witness to your life, for every dream you have ever had, and above all for wanting to be a better person. The steps you are taking today will bring the full manifestation of a new life and that is when your dreams will become real.

Rev. Rina A. González

Your life is not a dress rehearsal, live each moment as a first. Live your life knowing that you are that precious spark of divinity that came to experience life and that without you, we would miss how much you shine. Enjoy life knowing that it can only get better, for indeed it will!

Life is a Dance: Dance It!

When you pray, God stands.
When you stand and pray, God dances.
When you pray and dance,
God and you are one!

Hindu Wisdom

In order to have rhythm in life one needs to take a series of steps. If you like dancing or have ever danced, then you know that dancing is moving your body to the rhythm of the music followed by the ability to lead or follow. When leading or following are done in disproportion, you are either ahead or behind the music making the flow of the movements uneven. When life is lived in disproportion, the inability to balance one's life, makes the person ungraceful. This leads to falling short from receiving life's blessings.

Whether on the dance floor or going about your everyday life, a sense of balance should be present so that your actions are in harmony with your nature. When you are in rhythm with your nature, you are graceful, genuine and by all accounts, your life is blessed. If you are not, then change what you are doing wrong so that your life can become graceful, genuine, and blissful. Giving and receiving are the same as obeying of listening. The following are some of the meanings of obeying:

- To follow
- To comply
- To act upon
- To observe
- Abide by

- Conform to

    As we know, everything done for the first time seems foreign. Yet, as one work on the task that is before us, the seed of enlightenment awakens within and the subject matter is learned, understood, and put into practice in ones life. This is how spiritual lessons are learned; for that matter, this is how every thing is learned. When a wise person is working on a new topic and does not know or understand, inevitable the person seeks help. Usually the person calls a friend or colleague who is familiar with the subject matter. In spirit, the same thing is done, except the one we call upon is our Higher Self. Whether you know it or not, you already do, except talking under your breath and getting the answer you need, is given another name, such as 'coincidence', among others.

    Anytime you are speaking under your breath or are trying to recall the name of something or someone, the one you are contacting is your Higher Self and/or your Higher Mind. When you do, soon thereafter, the answer comes and instead of saying thank you, you think yourself to be a genius. By the way, we all have the potential to be geniuses, except we have to practice at getting good at it. That is how easy contacting spirit is. Now imagine calling your Higher Self or your Higher Mind consciously and think the results that doing this can bring you.

    Spiritual Guidance is felt or perceived by our senses:

- Feeling
- Touch
- Smell
- Sight
- Hearing
- Clairvoyance
- and Balance

The Contract of the Soul ~ Revised Edition 2011

It is through the senses that spirit contacts you and developing your senses and using them consciously will take you to experience the life you want to have.

I am often asked, how does one know that what they hear comes from spirit? Spirit's voice is easy to recognize, yet because of ego's chatter, it goes undetected by the untrained ear. Ego's voice is noisy, loud, opinionated, obstinate, and rude. Ego has no shame, knows no boundaries, can, and will lead you down the wrong path. Spirit's voice is like a breath of fresh air that gives you a knowing which, instinctually can be recognized. Ever hear the saying; I know beauty when I see beauty! Spirit's voice or its message is the beauty you want to embrace. The sages say that a man becomes wise by acting upon hearing spirit's voice.

You will find that following spirit's call will make your life a more enjoyable experience. All that you are being asked to do is to trust what is real in your heart, in your soul and in your entire being. If something does not resonate within you, don't do it, no matter who asks or tells you to do it. But if what I am giving you, resonates within your being then it behooves you to be wise and do it.

What I am asking you to do is to learn to trust what is real in you, that which is alive inside of you. Trust your essence, which is everywhere as is in, and all around you. Trust in what you are, knowing that only good can come your way.

Never stop learning or using what is at your fingertips. Asking for help is one of your many blessings. The opportunity of hearing, listening, and acting upon spirit's voice is one of life's greatest rewards. Know that the more you use your spiritual gifts and trust your instincts, the better that you will understand the message and interpret its' meaning.

Rev. Rina A. González

Now that you have read this lesson and more or less have the hang on it let me ask you this. Would you like to dance? If the answer is yes, why not practice what you have learned thus far and dance your life away? Remember that it is in obeying spirit's call that life will be an enjoyable experience and in doing what comes naturally is that you will find the Kingdom of Heaven within your very realm!

Non-Acceptance

"Those who deny caste are themselves forming a caste. Those who deny religion are themselves forming a religion. Even those who know much become prejudice against what they don't know or understand and when they talk against 'something new or different' they themselves are as ignorant as those who they've criticized. This behavior can only make us weak."

Santhya Sai Baba

Not accepting life for what life is, only complicates matters. By not accepting people, places and things for what they are, denotes arrogance, intolerance, and ignorance. This state of mind creates disharmonies in the body, hardens the heart arteries, and consequently stifles the creativity of the individual. Those who are intolerant of others ignore that the underlying energy behind this finite point of view is fear of the unknown, personal shame and guilt.

Taking this irrational view brings crippling consequences. And what is worse, after a lifetime of not <u>accepting life for what it is,</u> changing this point of view becomes hard, even impossible to achieve. The thing is that you are already perfect, in reality, we all are. Not knowing our perfection is what gives way to accepting what we are not. Accepting that you are imperfect, or saying that what is happening in your life is not of your doing denotes ignorance of the worse kind. Not accepting your brothers and sisters as equally denotes arrogance and this brings disharmony into your life. If your thoughts are not in harmony, if your words are not of peace, if your actions lack discipline and compassion towards all life form, how do you expect to get anything else but the same disharmony, lack of love and intolerance back in your life? A confused state of mind comes from a misunderstood thought, word, or action. Having a confused mindset can be easily correct by allowing clarity to enter the mind. However, in the absence of clarity, know that non-acceptance will reign supreme in all you think, say, and do. When you see yourself as an imperfect being, you will always find flaws and blemishes in everyone around you. Know that in doing this, all you have done is taint your perception and unless this is changed, in time your erroneous thinking will reassure you that indeed everyone is as imperfect as you think yourself to be.   Now, imagine how boring life would be, if everyone's was the same and we all had the same color skin, the same color hair, the same color eyes, same nose, same height, and same weight. We would all have the same thoughts, and would even like the same music. Now imagine that because of our likeness, conversation would be obsolete. Can you hear the deafening silence? Let us take this exercise one-step further and let us imagine that we all dressed alike, drove the same cars, and even had the same lifestyles and professions. Can you imagine the impact 'our likenesses' would have on the world's economy? Very little trade would take place because of this finite point of view. Life would become boring, to say the least, and surely no one would have the will or purpose to pursue or aspire to doing anything. Why dream of having a better life? Why dream of building a better world? For that matter, why live?

In our arrogance, ignorance, and limiting view of ourselves, we criticize those who are different from us without realizing that if we could change them to be more like us, the likeness itself would cause our world to come to a screeching halt. Not to mention that thinking of others as different from us infers that we think of ourselves as superior to 'to others', when in reality this is not true.

If this is how you think, I have a question for you; who

died and made you king? Individuals who think this way are bigots and their unwilling to change makes them barbaric. These individuals do not allow anyone around them to better their lives. They rather have an empty existence than to change their finite point of view. All righty then, can you answer these questions?

1. If we were all the same, from whom would we learn?
2. If everyone on the planet were the same, from whom would we learn the valuable lessons of compromise, compassion, and adaptability?

Let us not forget that there is nothing more stimulation than to have a civil debate among those with opposing view. You would be surprise at how much can be learned from listening to others. If we were all the same, then what would happen to the debate teams in our schools, colleges, and universities? Has it ever occurred to those with limiting views that all we have ever had and will continue to have are relationships? Who are you going to have a meaningful relationship with if you close your mind to spontaneity? After all, it is from having relationships that we learn, grown and become independent thinkers and hopefully, rational mammals.

Every soul is perfect, our imperfection comes from the untrained mind. Is a matter of fact, allowing our imperfections while doing nothing to change our present state, says a lot of the individual's character. For your soul to shine, you need to allow the perfection of the soul to unite with your humanity. Until this is achieved, you are demonstrating that you are incapable of obtaining your spiritual perfection. Perfection implies that your humanness reflects your souls perfection and not the other way around.

Right now, humanity is learning to stop killing its fellowman over stupid things like a plot of land or the oil found in its soil. Everyone says they want peace, yet man goes after what is not his, claiming to have the right to what is not, nor will it ever be. No one possesses anything that is material in nature. No one ever will.

The solution to our present dilemma is for each individual to find the flaws in their personality and work to eliminate said flaws by changing how and what they think, say, and do. Until then, our actions indicate that we are children of a lesser god. Wanting to have a better live without working to have one is not reasonable, intelligent and in reality is ludicrous. No perfection has ever been accomplished by a mere wish. Thinking that you are deserving of having a good life, when your life demonstrate the opposite, only comes from a deranged mind. If you, if any one of us, were already manifesting perfection in our lives, then the need to have wars would end.

If we were already perfect, then we would not have to learn anything new not would we have to change anything. This would mean that our actions would come from love, joy, peace, harmony, health, and prosperity. And because of our perfection, our world would be full of kindness and compassion allowing the perfection of being to be all around us. Our thoughts, words, and deeds would create miracles instead of catastrophes.

We have to be honest with ourselves and see that our present state does not reflect perfection. If you doubt this, then look at life on Planet Earth and see what our collective greed, lack of love and compassion has brought us. We, all humans inhabiting Planet Earth, have compromised our wellbeing by not loving or accepting our fellowman for whom and what he or she is.

At times, I wonder if closed-minded individuals use scare tactics in order to keep things the way they are, not so much, because they fear change but because they fear the unknown. News flash ~ today is the tomorrow you worried about yesterday and unless change comes, you will keep getting the same poor results and will end up creating more pollution for the whole of humanity. Pollution of mind, body, and of spirit equals pollution in our lives as well as in our planet. Based on what I see, Mother Earth needs a well-deserved respite from the lack of respect we have shown towards all life form.

So how about it, could we do something nice for a change and accept those that are different from us by letting them live their lives? How boring life would be if we were all the same? How insane and unjust life would be for those who hold their differences as badges of distinction and honor. Our differences should be treasured and shared with others. No one should ask another human being to caste aside their heritage to appease those who are intolerant of their roots or ignorant of their traditions and legacy. Can you not see that our differences make us stronger?

Much can be learn from our differences. A healthy debate increases the possibilities of understanding diversity among people, much faster than opposing it ever will. Different cultures expand our horizon. Gaining access to doing things in a different way allows us to be more in tune with our world. When you allow diversity to be your strong suit you will find that compassion is part of our nature for it is inherent in our humanity. To think that diversity is not our greatest strength is foolish. Diversity is what makes the world go round. Different ways of doing things is what creates growth in every economy. Without diversity, we would be at a lost and yet because of it, some people are unhappy and even think that 'their world' is ending. We can solve this problem right now.

Change your fixation on others having to be more like you by accepting people for who they are, and for what they do, and you will see how fast your internal struggles ceases. Accepting people for what they are will eliminate 99.9% of current social clashes. Thus, accepting people for what they are and for what they do, will allow you to let go of the preconceived idea of how life should be.

Scientists believe that over population is the cause of the world's upheavals. While this view has its merits, seeing it from a spiritual standpoint know that in reality the world's devastation comes from what 'humanity', emits onto the air {Prana, Ether}. Our lack of love and our intolerance towards life itself is at the core of our world's present upheaval. By acting hatefully towards our fellowman and by allowing our thoughts, words, and deeds to be lawless we are contributing to the making of catastrophic events. What is of importance here, is that acting this way only demonstrates how little respect we have for ourselves.

Last time I checked, we are all aboard our mother ship and if she goes down, we all perish. Not to mention that in acting so poorly we are denying our only truth to shine. Please remember that we are souls having a physical experience that came to earth to learn thus evolve. Rest assured that not wanting to learn from others or not wanting to share our love and compassion with others is at the root of all social injustice. Your need to change others comes from not wanting to see that the one who needs to change is you.

The Egyptians, before dying asked these two questions of themselves:

1. Did I have joy in my life?
2. Did I give joy to others?

What would your legacy be? How do you want to be remembered? By doing nothing, or by being part of the movement that will bring about the much-needed change to our lives and world? Remember that our children follow our footsteps, after all, they are the rightful heirs of the world. Therefore, it is our responsibility to make sure that the world we leave them is thriving in peace, love, abundance, and every possible opportunity.

Let our legacy to our children be love. Let us leave our children a world where getting along with one another is what is valued and our only difference is our home address and phone number.

May the human race take matters into their hands and may our resolve be to love and honor each one of our fellow man as our equal. Let us dare to change the course of our destiny by allowing the energies of peace, love, and understanding be present in all that we think, say, and do.

Let this be what we leave our children. Let us make the right choice, by eradicating hate, and bias from our vocabulary, thoughts and more importantly from our hearts, minds, and consciousness. Let us give Peace a Chance!

Rev. Rina A. González

*The Sun being the Sun has its blemishes.
The grateful see the light, the ungrateful see the blemishes.*
Pancho Villas

To Live Again
A Sonnet to Jesus

I kneel before you in reverence
Remembering all the good that has been lost.
Giving thanks for all of my sorrow
And for all of the miracles bestowed.

I merge onto your saintly image
Present in my soul that has been healed.
The constant love that I proclaim
Grows by day and by night becomes real.

As a child I asked you to guide me
Today see that the path is before me,
With roses all blooming in springtime
As they cover the past that's behind me.

With aroused enthusiastic happiness
My desire exposes its zealous.
As the love that's in me awakens
And my life is transformed into heaven.

There is vastness in our relationship
For you've asked me to love just for being.
It matter not what others may do
For by choice I do follow your image.

I've become stronger and wiser
By allowing my nature to shine.
I've been led to proclaim my divinity
And triumphantly be in your arms.

Rev. Rina A. González

When in doubt have call out for guidance
I have felt your present beside me.
As I breath have found your embrace
Transforming all doubt into gladness.

When fear has come to my life
You have answered the call in an instant.
I have felt your presence within
Making each atom of life become reason.

I know you are real for I've felt you.
And have seen you in the flowers as they sleep.
When they open their petals, I can smell
The fragrance of love that's deep within.

Heaven's nobility, I am moved
To see the sun's beauty through your eyes.
I sing to your holiness and might
From the depth of my soul; I am sublime.

I sing to the splendor of the night
When in rapture it erodes and gives the moon,
Her bright light that she shines upon the world
As her passion uncurls, becoming full.

I want to thank you for being a true friend,
For allowing me to gaze into your eyes
For I see that my dream is coming true
In spite of the blunders of the past.

For if in order to know who I've become
I need to go back and live life over,
Proudly I would turn and walk again

The Contract of the Soul ~ Revised Edition 2011

The same steps that brought me to your shoulders.

Knowing, that at the end of the journey,
Present, in each page already written,
There you will be, strengthening my soul,
To the constant beat of my unfoldment.

With my Love and Gratitude!

Rev. Rina A. González

Working the Soul Contract

I am a messenger and an instrument of peace!

In this section, the various clauses of our spiritual contract will be covered. Remember that what is offered in this book is learning to have a better life by understanding your spiritual heritage and powers. This book is not a cure all or a magic potion that will start to work the moment you start reading the book. While I am happy to know that my words resonate with you, work needs to be done in order for the change you want to come into your life. As you toil, as you learn to work with your spiritual gifts, a new awareness will be born. And as you discover how powerful you truly are, the new life you seek will emerge. As you start to change the way you think, speak and act the vibratory rate of your body will shift from low to high, from dense to light; and that is when old habits can be made anew.

Word of caution; do not attach yourself to any aspect of your new life for this soon will change. Enjoy the process knowing that the best is yet to come. The last thing you need is to create an expectation or an attachment to what you are experiencing when you are in the process of learning, evolving, growing, ascending, and mastering yourself.

If a new sensation arises, one that is unfamiliar to you, call your Guardian Angel and ask for clarity, this eliminates confusion. Remember that you are in the process of learning, changing, and evolving and not until you are finished doing the required work will you be able to make claims to anything or call a new experience a permanent one. Each experience is part of your awakening and every new experience teaches something different about the person you are becoming.

In fact, nothing in this book is new. Nor can I say that any thought, word, or action is new either. You, I, and all of us are using the same thoughts, words, and actions that were used by those before us. We can say that our actions are propelled by the imprints of long ago. What we are learning to do is qualifying our thoughts, words, and actions so that our lives can have a deeper awareness, a deeper meaning, one that will bring the life we truly want to have.

The lessons that I offer, were taught by the Wise Man and Sages in every previous civilization. I have nothing new to give you, nor do I think that there are new steps to give. However, following these steps will give you the life you seek only when you work towards understanding your spiritual nature. While this undertaking is not a difficult one, there are those think that a complete analysis is required before commencing any new task. These individuals do not see that 'Analyzing Paralyses'. Thinking wrongly is what brought you here. Stop thinking so much and just do it.

The following will come in handy:

1 CUP OF:	I REALLY WANT TO DO THIS
1 CUP OF:	WILLINGNESS
& 2 CUPS OF:	COMMITMENT TO MY NEW LIFE

Add all the ingredients in a crystal bowl, stir with a wooden spoon and start playing the game of life. Something that while you have heard before, you have never stopped long enough to ponder on what the game implies, nor have you used your spiritual tools correctly while playing the game of life. As you do, in time you will become aware that asking for guidance from your source is the right thing to do as also seeing that finding answers and understanding life's issues come to you easily as if by second nature.

Do not anticipate what is to come or make assumptions as to what the outcome will be. Let the moment take you to find its true meaning. Do the task for the love of the task itself, for this is the secret of experiencing the true moment; 'the present'. As everything else, the more you work on yourself, the better the results will be. Do not complicate things. Let life flow easily and in rhythm with your nature. As long as you are doing the required work willingly and are present in your life, change will come your way in no time at all for in reality, it has to.

Change is an inevitable event and when you seek it, change comes peacefully and abundantly. Allow your spirit to soar to new heights by expanding your wings and daring to fly higher than you have ever flown before. Clear your mind and let go of desired outcome and in its place bring forth the things that really matter to you. Make sure that the things you bring into your life are things that are deserving of been part of your new life's experience. Take the time to see what is standing in the way of you having a better life by shedding light on the obstruction. Obstruction impairs reasoning and limits growth. Shedding light happen when you go towards what ails you from the center of love, wisdom, and power, {your heart} and by applying light, the obstruction is removed. Remember that you are the light that came into the world. Use your spiritual powers correctly, lovingly and wisely. As time goes by, you will notice that peace is present in everything you think, say, and do. Enjoy the feeling of peace and be grateful for the experience.

Be the peace you feel and love all that has life. Feel the happiness that peace brings you, be grateful for your health, for being adventurous of spirit, for having a determined heart, and thank yourself for your courage. Do something special for yourself every day, especially after working on understanding your loving nature. Don't forget to smile and keep on reaching for the stars. Let me be the first to congratulate you for wanting to achieve enlightenment. Keep up the good work knowing that the best is yet to come!

The Contract of the Soul ~ Revised Edition 2011

Inspirational Thoughts

1. Nothing in excess brings happiness or joy. To experience true happiness know thyself first and all else will follow.
2. Man's only obligation in life is to comply with his personal legacy. It is obtaining clarity of mind that man is lead to see his purpose and in obeying spirit's call is that man is lead to find the key to his own emancipation.
3. Do not waste precious energy on the small stuff; instead, focus your unlimited potential on what you want to experience and all your needs will be met.
4. Not accepting people, places, and things for what they are, brings difficulties to your life.
5. In our universe, error is not a possibility.
6. The awakening of the critical mass starts with the awakening of the individual.
7. Live the ordinary life in a non-ordinary way.
8. Do the task for the love of the task itself; this is the secret to experiencing the true moment, the present; your gift.
9. "When you see the possibility of realizing your dreams is when life becomes interesting. And by allowing your spirit to soar is when your dreams become your reality."
10. "To me Life is Simple, and the Universe, Compassionate."

Rev. Rina A. González

"Change is inevitable and within your reach.
Be at peace with everything and everyone.
In time, the power within you will awaken
Transforming your very existence.
This is not only your heritage, it is your inescapable truth."

Rev. Rina

Playing the Game of Life

I am the resurrection and the life!

  The game of life begins the moment one enters the world and every experience comes from having relationships. We have a relationship with everything and with everyone, including money. Is a matter of fact, the person who lacks money is the one who is always thinking of having it; the rich never think of it, yet enjoy having it. The need to have what is lacking creates a fixation, and this is what keeps you from enjoying a wealthy and opulent life.

  Have you ever wondered what your relationship with creation is? Is it peaceful, joyous, agreeable, stable, and harmonious or are these attributes absent from it? Based on the relationships you have with yourself, with life and with creation is how all other relationships will be, including with money!

  We can safely say that life is based on relationships and that said relationships would be based on the individuals state of mind, feelings, and consciousness. Everything that comes to us was created by us. Our creations are nothing more than thoughts or wishes that escape us and go on the ether. We attract our manifestations or bring them down from the ether with our thoughts, words, and actions.

  Our most intimate relationship is the one who have with our mate. The most difficult of all relationships is the one we have with our children. And the tenderest of all relationships is the one we have with our parents. That is after we come to accept that all they ever did was obey our instructions set forth in the contract of the soul that everyone agreed to and signed before conception.

Now that we have touched upon the subject of relationship, let us suppose that you are having a hard time understanding what is happening to your mate. Of late, you feel that the energy has changed in the relationship and nothing you do makes your mate happy. Let me ask you this; who made you the keeper of your mate's happiness? This in it of itself might be creating the problem that you are encountering.

In trying to understand what might be wrong with your mate, you are focusing on what you are perceiving as wrong with him or her, while failing to see that who needs to change the perception on the matter, is you. Every time your attention is placed on other than what truly concerns you, is what will intensify, and in time, will manifest.

Your mate is responsible for his or her feelings, thoughts, words, and actions, as you are responsible for yours. You have never been nor will you ever be responsible for anyone else other than yourself. Nor will you ever be held accountable for what others say or do. However, you are responsible for what you perceive when others speak or act.

Your children will cease to be your responsibility the moment they demonstrate having the abilities to make a life for themselves. You can guide your children; you can lead them down your chosen path, knowing that ultimately it is up to them to follow their own. As far as your children listening to your advice, the answer is obvious.

Your job is to give advice, which in no way means that your children will follow your suggestion. Your responsibility as a parent ceases as your children are able to take care of themselves. A parent should cut the umbilical cord thus letting go of any attachments to the children and see him or her as an adult. Learn to accept what your adult child has chosen for themselves in their private lives.

In life, situations will arise, yet if your energies are balanced, **no - thing** can ever take you away from your center long enough to create disharmonies. Taking time to find something wrong with your mate is a clear sign that something is wrong with you. All that your mate is doing is pointing to what needs to be healed inside yourself.

Contaminated energy could be what is influencing the relationship negatively. If your home is not peaceful, there is the possibility that contaminated energy is the cause of the unrest. Contamination alters the results by influencing what we think, perceive, and feel.

<u>Energy is all that is</u> and as such, your home has the character trait of the different personalities that live in it. When someone in your home is unbalanced, their contaminated energy will affect and influence everything around them. All who are contaminated react to the unbalanced energy and though no one knows why, everyone feels the unrest as well as pays the consequences. If you think that this could be happening in your home, then may I suggested that you check the energy for blockages around the house. If blockages are present, remove them. Make sure that all corners are free from any obstruction. A good energy cleansing, at home, business or on an individual soothes all relationships. You will notice that when your atmosphere is clean the home, air, and ambiance become cleaner, crisper, smoother, and fresher. It also helps if you become organized. Anything that is broken, especially glass, plumbing or electrical appliances, fix them. If your finances are in disarray, create a budget and stick to it. Do not go over the budget for any reason. Focus on the abundance and prosperity that is already yours knowing that in time, it will come. When you focus on scarcity this is what you will manifest.

Word of caution: Do not waste valuable time in going over the issue. If the energy in your home is contaminated it needs to be cleaned, and if you do not know how to do it, then find someone who does.

Pay the practitioner their fee and do not ask for a discount, nor should you do any kind of bartering in exchange for their services. Discounting or bartering with your life or the wellbeing of your loved ones is foolish. You are too precious not to honor the work of others, especially when it has to do with removing blocked energy from your home, place of business or from a dear one. The saying, "penny wise pound foolish" comes to mind.

****

We came well equipped to be victorious in life. As I know that, we have to find our own unique path in life. No event is better or worse than any other, because each one of us has the power to change any event into what we want it to be. "Good Luck and Good Fortune" is nothing more than the ability to hear what resonates within your soul and once the message is understood, make it your reality. If this is what you already do, then you have Good Luck and you are a Very Fortune Individual.

Using "The Contract of the Soul" in your everyday life is the same as using a secret passage to your own emancipation or having the 'good fortune' of having personal guidance from spirit to resolve pending issues. "And I say unto you, Ask, and it shall be given you; seek, and you shall find; knock, and it shall be opened unto you." These words are real because they are alive within you. Use them wisely and as you do, you will get smarter about 'this thing called life' as the answers you seek appear before you very eyes.

The Contract of the Soul ~ Revised Edition 2011

Voyage to the Unknown

"To me Life is Simple, and the Universe, Compassionate."
Rev. Rina

In life, nothing happens by chance and every lesson takes us to a greater awareness of the self. Coming to the see that, 'what I see in others is simply my own reflection' was a breathe of fresh air. Understanding that every one around me is a teacher was very revealing. Yet, before I knew this, played the game of pointing the finger, anytime something went wrong in my life. The things that used to upsets me about others, were nothing more than dark aspects of myself that I had not worked on, did not know had, or had not understood.

It is clear that no one walks with a mirror hanging from their neck therefore, it can be said that we do not know what we do. If we did, we would see our flaws and correct the old habits that keep us from having a better life. Since we do not see our flaws and for all practical reasons are unaware of having any flaws, we need those around us to show us what is wrong or what needs to be fixed. How do we see in others what we need to fix in ourselves? The only way that we can understand that something needs to be fixed or changed is by seeing in others that same dark aspect of ourselves and not liking it.

What is even more interesting is that the other person might not have the flaw, yet you see it in him or in her as a reflection of your own flaw. When you see goodness in others, it is because there is goodness in you. And when you see negative traits in others, it is because you have the negative traits.

Life's lessons are learned by having experiences. Our experiences come from having relationships. Our perception uses our senses to identify the feelings associated to what we see, hear, taste, smell, or touch. Therefore, your life is base on your perception. Make no mistake about this. It is from using the senses that your world turns. And as you know, only one-perception counts, and that perception is none other than yours.

Perception is an insight by which discernment enters your awareness. Discernment creates an opinion about what you see, hear, taste, smell, or touch. From your perception, an opinion is formed and this becomes your mental image. In turn, this mental image is recorded in the mind, the cells, and the subconscious. From that moment on, whether you are right or wrong, unless the image is changed, the mental image that you hold, will dictate what you will do, and how you will feel any time the memory of the event that created the image arises.

Paying close attention to your feelings and understanding them is how you will become sensitive to spirits voice. Interpreting the information so that what you perceive is coded correctly will make life easier. Sensitivity creates compassion, sympathy, understanding, kindness, and tenderness. By observing these spiritual traits and by developing them, is how your humanity will merge with the soul making them inseparable, allowing them to become one. This closeness, this perfect union will bring you the perfection of being.

The meanings of the <u>word discernment</u> are:
- Judgment
- Acumen
- Discrimination
- Perspicacity

- Sensitivity

Energy is all that is. Energy is what we perceive in its various forms, around us as well as in others. However, when your lens is dirty, you can only perceive incorrect information and in turn, the information you perceive becomes contaminated. Therefore, all information stored in the mind, cells and sub-conscious is contaminated. Energy enters our awareness free of any contaminant, attachment, or judgment. Then who, if not you, is responsible for contaminating clean energy with your wrong impressions of others?

An illusion is a false impression or a misapprehension caused by an interaction with something or someone. This false impression is captured by the individual's perception and is coded incorrectly. And even though what took place does not merit a conflict, to the person who perceived it incorrectly, sees it as a reason to have a conflict. Until this is changed, you can only get the same impure images that you are holding. Wars have started because of this absurdity and thousands of lives have been lost because of a false impression. Illusions bring confusion and confusion creates more of the same.

Repeatedly, lessons, which are intended to enrich ones life become problematic in nature, only because they have been made to be something other than what they truly are.

Energy comes in and goes out of our awareness constantly. It is up to the individual to make sure that what he or she stores in their minds, cells and sub-conscious is deserving of been kept. As souls, we love adventure. The thing is that I do not see that much progress has been made. It seems that we keep missing the mark and perhaps that is the reason why we have come back so many times. To have an adventure is a good thing, is a matter of fact, adventures are fun. So why being adventurous souls, have we allowed our human imperfections to create havoc in our lives?

Rev. Rina A. González

While humanity has managed to go from having four legs and crawling to walking upright and having a thumb, our cells still carry the spark of un-forgiveness that has caused grief and destruction to all life form on Planet Earth.

Yes! Humanity has learned to use its vocal cords, it is able to speak different languages and dialects, yet the human race has not figured out how to communicate effectively, peacefully and amicably with its fellowman. Is this progress or is this another form of ignorance and arrogance in disguise?

While humanity has managed to conquer distant lands by making war a profitable business, what humanity has not done is conquer the self. We have gone to the depth of the mighty oceans, in search of God knows what, yet we cannot seem to find the depth of our soul. In our desire to explore all that is around us, man has traveled to the edge of our galaxy, has spent trillions of billions of dollars trying to find extra terrestrial life when we cannot figure out our lives. We keep failing to have the good life we say we want to have. Is this not insane and hypocritical behavior?

Whom we need to conquer, is ourselves. What we need to find is who we are. Our need to look outside ourselves will never cease unless we are willing to explore a new horizon within our very realm. We are the lost continent that we are searching for. We are the lost continent that has eluded us for far too long. What we are searching for is at our fingertips.

The continent of 'you' and 'me' and 'all of us', needs to be found, for until we do, we will keep on acting as children of a lesser god as well as being the lowest form of life in our galaxy. Life is a choice and learning to live your life peacefully among your fellowman is a choice that needs to be made consciously. Happiness is not only a choice it is your birthright. Be honest with yourself and see that change needs to be made. Then consciously take the first step towards making change happen in your life.

The Contract of the Soul ~ Revised Edition 2011

Unveiling Life's Mysteries

"When you see the possibility of realizing your dreams is when life becomes interesting. And when you allow your spirit to soar your dreams become your reality."

Rev. Rina

- *Personal*

- *Profession: Work / Business Relations*

- *Perfect Strangers*

- *Places and Things*

Before we proceed; it might prove to be wise if next time you are having a hard time dealing with those around you, know that pointing a finger to your immediate left, right, up, down, or across, come from not seeing that the only one you should be pointing to, is you. In addition, it might help if you remember that this person, place, or thing that is provoking you to react shamelessly has come to teach you a valuable lesson, perhaps the lesson of reasoning. Learn your lesson and get on with living your life!

Anytime anything or anyone causes you to react disharmoniously, YOU being the common denominator, should welcome the opportunity to heal that part of you that keeps you in the grips of ignorance. At times, life's lessons can be so painful, that the mere presence of this person, place, or thing might send a surge of negative energy through the entire body. Please know that leaving the room is recommended. It is better to excuse yourself than to create a scene. In truth, calling this person, place or thing names that only belong to you, will later lead to regrets. So relax and know that learning how to be free from your demons is part of life's curriculum. No one can learn your lessons for you, nor can you learn anyone else's lesson. You are responsible for learning what you signed up for. Any time you feel overwhelmed, it is because you have introduced someone else's lessons' into your energies. Learn to value and appreciate your teachers, those wonderful souls who keep showing up to teach you what you have refused to learn. You should appreciate coming to terms with the fact that every lesson's objective is to teach you to reason. This noble concept has remained illusive to many of us because of not accepting who and what we are {*a soul having a physical experience*} or how to create what we truly want to experience {*a happy and prosperous life*} or how to claim what is already ours *by working with our spiritual gifts properly.*

    Once you come to terms with what matters, not only will you start to notice that your experiences become more harmonious, but the mere fact of claiming ownership of your life, [being present in the moment, and making conscious decisions], the conscious act will grant you safe passage on the road to self-discovery. Being aware of your surroundings will help to heighten your spiritual powers, this takes you to understand life at a deeper level. From then on, when confronted with any disruption, you will know that this too shall pass and that putting things in perspective is smart.

    When will you stop learning? Hopefully never! I have come to see that the more I learn about life, the more I want to learn. After all, it is from learning, knowing and discerning that true growth can be achieved. As you get older, life becomes easier, but do not postpone learning for the golden years. Live life in the moment, love every experience life offers and above all make the conscious decision to learn something of value every day that you are alive.

The Contract of the Soul ~ Revised Edition 2011

It is my fondest wish that all the children of a loving universe get this living thing right, once and for all. If not, we would have missed the opportunity of being part of the betterment of our race.

Namaste!

Rev. Rina A. González

"As souls we are always moving towards a greater awareness of the self. We are always evolving, even though we might not be aware that we are. The child grew to become the adolescent. The adolescent became the adult. The adult in time turned in its youthful appearance for a serene look. Yet none of these changes caused you concern or sadness. Such is the power of evolution.

Be grateful for having an adventurous heart and enjoy the journey that takes you to discover the amazing wonders that you hold. May you joyously march to the beat of your unfoldment."

Rev. Rina

Parents Soul Contract

I live in the consciousness of love!

All that you will ever have are relationships and all relationships can be changed or modified to fit the person you are becoming. Abuse or lack of respect in any relationship should not be tolerated, by anyone at anytime. Yet in our society, both tendencies take many forms. Any form of abuse is reprehensible, however, when the abuse is committed towards a child, a child entrusted to you, to love, guide and protect, your actions go beyond culpability and demonstrate your lack of integrity as a fellow human being.

Children learn by example. When a child is abused off from an early age, the virgin clay that was born burns away leaving little room for improving or changing what has become habitual. In time, the abused child will become unruly, shy, and unfriendly, and eventually will abuse others. These children lack love for themselves so they love nothing and respect no one.

Look around you, take a good look at our youth, and ask yourself if as a person, an adult or as a parent, you have contributed to what our youth is presently experiencing. If the answer is 'yes', find a way to bring a peaceful resolution to the pitiful state that our youth is experiencing and do not stop until you have made every attempt to correct the wrong done.

In today's world, parents are so involved in doing what comes easiest that they have forgotten how to parent. Entire weeks go by without the family seating down to have a home cooked meal or a pleasant conversation around the dinner table. Today's parents seldom have rules for themselves so it tends to reason that they have no rules for their children. Sometimes these unruly children rule the home. This too is a form of abuse.

More and more children are involved in gang activities, both males and females are conducting themselves in ways that denote arrogance, greed, lack of love and have no respect for authority. Did you know that our children's behavior demotes the kind of parents we are? I am glad that my parents had such a strong sense of self, that not only did they take good care of us, their children, but also, they engraved in us the family motto. Our family motto was a subliminal message which said; "I brought you into this world and have the right to take you out." Funny, all five of us understood what the message meant and few dared to tempt fate.

Our parents loved us so much that they gave us everything in exchange for respect and obedience. Our home had rules and each one of us was taught these rules since early on. Among these rules were curfew, code of conduct, good morals, discipline, and good table manners. In our home, if you wanted to eat at the grown up's table, you had to display good manners, those of us who did not, did not eat with those that did. In our home, there were two tables, a big one in the dining room, and a little one in the kitchen. The grown ups and the children who had learned good manners, sat at the big table. While the children who had not learned how to eat properly, ate at the little table in the kitchen.

As a child, I never got upset at the fact that I could not be in the big table. Is a matter of fact, wanting to eat at the big table is why I learned to have good manners quickly so that I could. Funny thing, when my time came to teach my children, have to say, that they too have impeccable eating habits.

Today's youth does not know how to seat properly at a table nor do they know how to look at a person in the eyes or can they have a meaningful conversation with anyone. Now a days our youth have no ethics, no moral values, have terrible manners, and demonstrate not having any self-control. My question to the patents is; why did you have children, if you are doing a disservice to a soul and to the future adult?

Our parents made sure that we did not go to bed hungry, we were never malnourished, we had clothes on our back, and shoes on our feet. Our father spoiled us and our mother corrected the harm done by bringing us down from the cloud that our father had placed us on. I have come to see that a timely refrain has never killed anyone. This refrain is what the children in today's world are missing. No one in their lives has cared enough to let them know that there is a fine line between getting your way and not being able to.

As souls, our children choose their parents to guide them through life. Our job as parents is to give them the tools they will need in order to become individuals. Parenting has never been easy but it can become an enjoyable experience when we know that whom we have in our care is a precious soul. No soul will ever be the private property of anyone. We will never own a soul; how can an essence be anything but free to enjoy life fully. However, we do need to guide these souls with love, affection and discipline so that they can become all that they can be.

The job of a parent is to enrich our children's life by giving them unconditional love and by being the constant guidance, they need, even though they will refuse the two. In time even thought we think they were not listening you will see that indeed they were. You will even see them doing to their children, the same things they hated when it was done to them.

Your constant love and reassurance is all the security they need to grow. And when they open their wings to fly, make sure that you do not stop them with your inhibitions or insecurities. Instead, encourage them to fly higher next time.

And as they soar, remind yourself that from that moment on your job is to be the silent witness of whom they have

Rev. Rina A. González

become. Teach by example and always encourage them to follow their own path in life. Be a source of inspiration to your children by becoming all that you can be.

Trust that what you have given them will take them the rest of the way home. In time, you will see that you managed to do a good job. And even though they will never give you the much-deserved credit, give yourself a pad on the back and smile every chance you get, knowing that life does not any better than this!

The relationship between mother and child

*"I never did give anybody hell.
I just told the truth and they thought it was hell."*

Harry S. Truman

    Every relationship is meant to teach that as we love the flaws in others is that we find ourselves. Everything is life has an exception, yet accepting the unacceptable, makes everyone culpable. The relationship between a mother and her child is the strongest bond ever conceived. Yet, as precious as our newborns are, as they grow, some of us will experience unconceivable sorrow, torments, and regrets. What few mortals know or are willing to accept, is that this person for whom you would do anything for, in previous lives was your enemy.

    Here comes the interesting part. Depending on how deep the energy of hate runs within these individuals is what will determine the tolerance and resiliency of the mother. Her job is to improve, fix, or change the relationship by having the child learn the lessons of reasoning, acceptance, and guidance from the one person the child intensely dislikes.

    It is in this relationship that we can see the *Divine Plan* working to perfection. Not only does it bring closure to pending karmic debt between the two, but also this is when both, mother and child can learn to accept each other's imperfection and heal them by being kind, and compassionate towards the other.

    No matter what a child does, a mother is always ready to forgive by giving of her unconditional love to the child. The mother's labor of love is that of knowing that this too shall pass while the child's is to respect and honor. As we know not many children do this honoring thing very well and in some cases this form of non-compliance creates conflicts in the home.

And of course, there are extreme cases, as is the child kills its mother or the mother killing the child. When this happens there are those among us who ignoring what I am addressing, criticize vehemently the event, stating that they would never do such a thing. May I suggest that you start been honest with yourself by searching for the many times that underneath your breathe you felt like killing one of your children. I am honest enough to admit that I am one of the fortunate few who having had the thought never carried it out.

There are cases were the relationship between a mother and child is so out of control that to save what little is left the two part ways, until the animosities are under control, or at least a better understanding of what is taking place is reached by both parties. In our resent past, when a relationship between a mother and her child was not a good one, the child was send away to boarding school. Of course, the child ended hating the mother even more than before making visitation time intolerable for everyone. Finally, the child grew and went back home, where inevitably played the blaming game to the tune of using the mother's decision to send him or her away as the cause for their instability and unhappiness. What these individuals do not know is that the only reason why they are alive, or are not serving a lengthy prison term is because they were send away from the one person who could have killed them or whom they could have killed.

Of course, the mother sends the child away not knowing the underlying mysterious that I have explained here, all she knows is that the child acts out, is unruly, disobedient, impulsive, rude, and lacks compassion. She does not know or dare face the fact that she is the energy that propels the child's negative behavior, nor is she aware that she could harm the child. These events happen regularly. Throughout history, these occurrences do take place, yet socially these incidents are called flukes, when in reality, they are anything but.

This falls under the false impression that this too shall pass, when what we do not understand is that feelings are powerful energies and unless understood they can be destructive. What we fail to see is the origin or root [cause] of the energy by only looking at the behavior of the child or the mother [effect]. Unless this is understood, the same mistakes will be made.

Perhaps if we could learn to be more truthful with ourselves there would be no need to lie about disliking someone, even if this someone was your mother or your child. We have to come to understand that love and like are two different feelings. While we love the child, we might not like what the child does. It is okay not to like a disruptive behavior and we have the right to protect ourselves from what we do not understand or cannot help change. Is a matter of fact, this is considered a prudent act.

Please, understand that neither child or mother are aware why any of this is taking place, all they know is that it is. In severe cases, an outside source should assist as to bring a peaceful or amicable resolution between mother and child. There are those who seek spiritual guidance if this is what they practice, and of course, there are those who do nothing. Unfortunately, in the absence of logic instead of learning to love what is unlovable, the relationship will continue to deteriorate. At a soul level, if unresolved they have tied themselves cosmically for another round of birth-and-rebirth.

Perhaps reading this, mothers can come to understand the reason why without wanting to, there are times that we feel the way we feel or why our thoughts, although socially incorrect, we have them anyway.

Those who choose to clean their karma go through the fires of purification to transmute their imperfections in order to achieve their freedom from past mistakes. Having children is nothing more than learning another one of our lessons. However, this lesson makes you go farther than any other and is one that can take you to find the depth of your soul. however, it is important that we remember that we signed the contact agreeing to become better at this thing called life, and as life would have it, there is a successful conclusion to this unlearned lesson; learn it well and you will never again have another sleepless night in this one, or any other life.

I am certain that the love of the mother surpassed any other love. For the love of her child a mother, goes thought the excruciating pains of labor and moments after her child is born finds herself falling in love, deeper than ever before with a total stranger. Could it be that a mother's love and acceptance of her child is so strong that it can wipe all karmic debt between them? I am sure that it does.

What is even more amazing is that the honor of being a mother is bestowed only on the females of the specie. Every father, no matter what, is loved by their children while the mother has to prove herself to be worthy of her child's love. The mother's unconditional love for her child is what is of importance here, for the energy of love has the power to change everything.

How can a mother not love the child that she carried in her womb? How can she suffer the pains of labor, give life to another being, and not love? In this sublime instance is when the *Divine Plan* is carried out to perfection, and when what could not be accomplished in previous lives comes full circle. Yet ignoring the meaning of the moment is what prevents us from seeing that the karmic debt has been paid in full.

Foot Note:

I know myself to be a very fortune person and have many reasons to be grateful and thankful and I am. But the one that I am grateful the most for is the understanding that in this incarnation, I had the perfect mother.

No matter what she did or did not do, my mother always had my love and respect. Knowing that there is no criticism of self-righteous indignation against another female, makes me be an accomplished person, woman, daughter, and mother. As a soul, I am eternally grateful for knowing that because of our love, we conquered our fate and karma is forever clean between us.

May my children have my same fate. May they see in me the soul they chose as their mother in this incarnation, and may they learn to forgive all my shortfalls.

Rev. Rina A. González

Oriental Symbol for Happiness

Tell me and I will forget.
Show me and I might remember.
Involve me and I will understand.

Oriental Proverb

The Contract of the Soul ~ Revised Edition 2011

The contract between siblings

To make things as easy as possible to understand, we can summarize the four boundless qualities in the single phrase "a kind heart." Just train yourself to have a kind heart always and in all situations.

Patrul Rinpoche

From my siblings I learned the valuable lessons of courage, integrity, and forgiveness. Being courageous or strong does not mean having the power to bend the bow or the sight to aim and hit the target, but rather, it is a deeper sense or awareness, perhaps a knowing, that says; even though you could, you should not. Forgiveness is not a feeling of righteousness, but rather, an acceptance of what has happened, learning from what took place, and moving on with your life. In my estimation, this act is very noble and seldom will it be seen for what it is, especially by those who commit the heinous act.

Jose Martí, a Cuban patriot poet and writer, who for years have admired, and whose writings have had a profound impact in my life, said it best in this quote; *"To forgive, a good memory is required."* While numerous books have been writing about forgiveness, and countless others address sibling rivalry, making no claims to neither being, a physiologist or therapist, having had the experience of forgiven my siblings feel that this gives me freedom to write about the topic. Funny thing though, while I forgive my siblings for their trespasses, what I had not done, was forgive myself for allowing them to offend, hurt, taunt, or malign me. As I write this, I do so in the hopes of clarifying why things that should not happen, do.

To me, life is simple and too easily complicated by power struggles that this relationship creates. And let us not forget that in having this relationship is when we learn to point the finger at those around us. Funny thing, even though complicating my life was never my intention, felt that with my sisters I had to go the extra mile to make sure that I was understood. Of course having to do this created the confusion that I did not want to experience.

Did my sisters get me? To this day, I am not sure they ever did but to be perfectly honest, what my sisters think is none of my business my only concern is not allowing them to mistreat me. Perhaps what happened took place because that I am different than they are, and not knowing what to make of 'my difference' or with 'who I am', they opted to offend, hurt, taunt, and malign me, every chance they got. Was their behavior hateful? Yes. What was their motive? To be honest, I do not know, nor do I want to know. However, do know that they were full of fear, bias, and ignorance and perhaps this combination is the fuel that leads to be hateful.

When I started to write this book, while I knew of its content, did not know with specificity the subject matters that would be addressed. The farthest thing from my mind was that I would be using my life experiences as comparisons or examples of dos and don'ts. With time, have come to see that the only reason why we have experiences is to learn from them. And if there is anything that I have done well in this incarnation is learn to value life in every regard, as am glad that my conduct has been based not on what others do or do not do, but on my reaction should be.

The hand has five fingers, yet each digit is different and all five make the hand. The same holds true for my four siblings and me. I had a close relationship with my late brother Manny. Presently have a relationship with my older sister. When we were younger had difficulty seeing eye-to-eye in anything and because of our differences and unwillingness to bend, countless conflicts took place. Today see those conflicts were stupid, childish, unreasonable, and unnecessary, yet they happened nonetheless. Perhaps our relationship has improved, not because we are older, but because we have learned to tolerate each other's differences and have found that, our assets surpass our downfalls.

While the five of us were born from the same parents, the younger two are different. Maybe by the time they were born, our parents were tired of setting rules and did not have the strength to give them the same code of conduct that was embedded in the oldest three. Or instead of blaming my parents for my sisters actions, I can go on record and state that what happened between my two younger sisters and me is nothing more than pending karma.

Culturally, families are those to whom we are born onto. Spiritually know that the only one that can teach valuable lessons are those closest to us, those we love the most are the only ones that can get close enough to hurt us. Even though I felt that my two younger sisters envied me, what I never thought possible was that one day, they would betray my trust and love, yet they did. The sisters I loved and would have done anything for, betrayed me in the worse possible way.

My sanity and strength come from spirit. Throughout life, the constant has been searching for the truth within me. If I had found that I harvested disharmony towards either one of my two younger sisters, I would have apologized. Since none was found I have not, yet neither have they. I know that my karma is clean by the mere fact that I have not hurt neither one, before, during or after. The thought of knowing that my karma is clean gives me peace, for not only was an old score settled, more importantly, our paths shall never meet again.

Culturally, unity among family members its' sanctified. Of course, there are those who think that all uneventful events should be forgiven, yet what these individuals miss is that when sacred laws are broken and hateful and careless acts corrupt the fabric of our being, the relationship is not salvageable and the spiritual contract is null and void.

In metaphysics, there is the saying; *"when the pupil is ready, the teacher appears"* Sai Baba was a modern day saint who passed away recently in the South of India. I came across an article of his and as I read it, understood with whom to have a relationship and whom to avoid.

The article said. "One of Sai Baba's disciple was having difficulty with some of his relatives and during prayer time, asked Sai for guidance in regards to his predicament. Sai looked into the man's soul and after reaching his conclusion said. *"We are all children of the light. We all come from the light. Our brother the tiger, the lion, the serpent, they too come from the light, but you will not see me go into their den for I know that they will eat me."* Thank you Sai!

Soul Mates

Without a doubt, this is humanity's greatest misconception!

Rev. Rina

We have many soul mates; is a matter of fact we are all soul mates to one another. It should also be noted that due to our adventurous nature we splintered of away from our other half creating different aspects of ourselves throughout the universe and galaxy. However, there are souls that resonate more to us and the reason why is because in them we recognize part of ourselves and the closes of intimacy give us comfort. We have reincarnate and evolved with these souls through many lifetimes as is true that we have learned lessons in each one of our many unions and parings from one another.

It should be noted that not all our lessons are loving or comforting as is the lesson of forgiveness and that of unconditional love, for they can be challenging at times. Sometimes we are the "victim," and sometimes we are the "darkness," yet both aspect of the self shows or teaches us the lesson of going towards the light. We can say that this is when freewill and discernment plays a big role in our life.

Someone can come into your life and cause you pain and suffering, yet this is a soul with whom you have contracted and the lesson of pain makes you reflect and from both comes growth and evolution and if you choose to do, so lovingly forgiveness is your reward. Our greatest joy and our greatest pain are both conceived through engaging with our soul mates as feelings intensified depending on how strong the soul connections is, but know that whether the results are good or bad everything that happens you have agreed to the moment you signed your soul contract.

Rev. Rina A. González

We will often spot a soul mate or karmic relationship by what humans call "love at first site" or "revulsion at first site," depending upon the lessons you've contracted to learn from this soul. One can live a lifetime in joy and harmony with a resonant soul mate, yet this while beautiful is a rare gift.

"You are part of the Divine Creation. You are not alone and to get involved in your life all you have do, is be present in the moment."

Rev. Rina

The Contract of the Soul ~ Revised Edition 2011

Best Friend

*"A friend is someone who touches your hand
And without you knowing, takes your heart."*

Rev. Rina

What can be said about a gentle soul who walked among us and to whom, I had the privilege of calling brother? Those who knew Manny know of his soothing voice and how with a hug could uplift your spirit. Those who have yet to meet him will soon learn why to me he was and is my best friend.

Manny was the only boy born to the González García family. For the time allotted, we had the privileged of sharing our experiences with him. Upon his passing, we were left longing for his presence and know that to this day we all miss his unforgettable essence, heart, and soul.

While being the only boy in the family to some might seem advantageous, Manny never allowed our favoritism for him go to his head. Actually, he did not like anyone fussing over him. Manny was a unique individual and even though he loved everyone he was never concerned with the small stuff. Manny did not worry if you agreed with him, or if you liked what he had to say. Regardless of your opinion, he did what needed to be done, and said what needed to be said.

He was funny, clever, a constant explorer of life, an inventor with an adventurous spirit. He never forgot how to be a child and encouraged us to experiences life the same way by being free to experience the unexpected. He did all this with a smile on his face, a cigarette in his mouth and a bottle of rum by his side.

There are many stories about Manny; however, want to share his last act of, knowing that it speaks volumes of the depth of his soul.

Upon realizing that he was dying, he made the conscious decision to contact everyone he had ever known and to each of those individuals he posed the same question. Have I ever offended you?

Those whom he asked were stunned to hear the questions and tried to reassure him that he had never offended them. However, Manny would not have their sympathy and inevitable added, "I know I that am dying as I know that I have made mistakes, reason why I am asking you to forgive me for anything I might have done to hurt you. Know that if I did, those were never my intentions."

As you can imagine there was not a dry eye in the house yet, know that everyone benefited from Manny's determination to settle old scores. He even asked the same question to my then, 5-year-old granddaughter. And while she could not understand why Manny was asking her this, he did not let her go until she had kissed him and had said that she loved him.

Funny thing, he never asked me that question. For a long time I did not understand why, until one day it dawned on me; Manny and I never had pending karma, before during or after. I am grateful that he was my brother and that we were friends. He was the person I could go to when I needed a shoulder to cry on, as he could with me. Manny was my rock, his words at times might have been harsh yet know that his intentions were meant to wake me up.

No matter what the situation was, we were there for each other even if we disagreed with what the other one was doing or saying. Our unconditional love knew no mental reservation, had no judgment, and was so strong that we could be free to be ourselves in the presence of the other knowing that the we had each other's back.

When we were kids our mother could relax when we disagreed, {we kept to ourselves} but could not when we got along well, only because we got into trouble frequently. Yet both our parents knew that we were kids having fun. While we had many adventures, one is very fitting. Manny and I had vivid dreams and as children do, we told each other the dreams from the previous night. One day realized that there was one dream in particular that Manny and I shared. In this particular dream, both of us had the same experience of flying over a great big mountain and then dropping into its precipice yet knew that nothing would harm us.

Both of us liked the felling of being free to fly and we had that when we had this dream. The more we had the dream, the more that we confided our experiences with the other. I observed the *coincidences within the dreams*, {coincidence is a mathematical equation that means that what is happening is perfect}, which were:

- We only had this particular dream on Thursday's
- We both enjoyed the experience
- We recognized the landscape when the other narrated the dream

One day I said to him. Why don't we ask to taken to our mountain next Thursday, that way we can fly there together. We agreed and before going to sleep the following Thursday reminded each other of our meeting that evening. We meet that night and many nights after that. In time, we become experts at playing a game that captured our imaginations. Of course, neither one of us knew that what we were doing was inconceivable to others. All we knew was that our desire to fly allowed us to go to a place we liked and felt good while there. Today I know the name of this place and it is none other than, 'the field of all possibilities.'

Rev. Rina A. González

Our innocence and determination had done what to others is not possible and for a moment in time, two children were able to express the lightness of their souls at play. This happened because we trusted each other and together dared go beyond *'all social conditioning'* and allowed our Guardian Angels to lead the way.

Thanks Manny, see you in my dreams!

Manny & I having a conversation at the tender ages of 6 & 7. Priceless!

The Contract of the Soul ~ Revised Edition 2011

To be happy, find your passion
In your profession, work or business

In all activities, train the mind through meditation.

  Whether you are a professional who earned a degree from college, a university or trade school, unless passion is involved in what you do, all you have is a *j.o.b,* which lacks the passion to motivate you which will never make you happy or can it be fulfillment. I do not care how much money you make at your *j.o.b*. I do not care how prestigious your title is either. Unless what you are doing makes you happy, sadness will overwhelm you and eventually your choice will make you sick.

  The truth is that it is not difficult to discover what your passion in life is. For one, it is what you do instinctively and you do it with great ease, doing it brings you happiness, relaxation and you love to share it with others.

  What is more, what you like to do you has never had to go to school to learn how to do it. You do it as if by second nature. So why I wonder don't you find to way to turn what you are passionate about into a business, and in the process of doing what you love to do make money, be happy and the tranquility, peace and joy that your passion will bring you will restore your health to full perfection.

Love's Embrace

Dare to dream by finding the joy in life.
Dare to go after what you have always dreamed.
You will never regret having ventured into splendor
or embracing the love that is within your loving heart!

Rev. Rina

Rev. Rina A. González

The perfection in what's strange

With unfailing kindness, your life always presents what you need to learn. Whether you stay home or work in an office or whatever, the next teacher is going to pop right up.
Charlotte Joko Beck

There is a simple definition to "space/time continuum," which is that space and time is the whole of one entity. Mathematically, Einstein explained his field equation thesis, by using the following definition for space/time continuum as:

"The space/time continuum is a collection of parametric specifications that attempt to define *'is.'* The specifications can be as single value and thus define a specific point in space/time, or they can be continuous and define an entire entity."

As you can see, truth is stranger than fiction. Seeing that this topic defies what humans call 'logic or reason,' I will try to clarify yours question. However, it might prove beneficial if those who are reading this realize that learning something new needs time to be digested, assimilated, and understood before jumping the gun and claiming to be the master of the new topic. For better understanding of how this theory works, it would be best if we were to associate it to life itself. In doing so, we might see that what *Einstein* explained is that humans are part of the same space/time continuum, reason why we are inter-connected, as well as inter-changeable energy who form the whole of creation.

This can only mean that life is a collection of space/time continuum events, which are all happenings at the same time and space. All incarnations and every life experience you have had, are taking place at the same time, continuously and simultaneously. This is how humans are connected to one another. It is in the acceptance of this truth, that you can come to understand the power of our human connection. This also explains why lost civilizations are so intriguing to us. Their proximity takes us to find them, as if we were looking for some lost parts of ourselves. Even more intriguing is the possibility that maybe those lost civilizations for whom we seek, are the ones contacting us, reason why we search for other life form outside our galaxy and beyond.

    Seeing that everything that exist in our universe is energy and that we are part of the whole of creation what stops us from using said energy to guide us through life? If we did, I am sure that our lives would be a wondrous experience. Think of how many strangers have come into your life for a brief moment. Why do you think that is? Who could they be if not someone with whom we have shared experiences in another life? These souls are loved ones from our recent past whose energies are still sketched in our souls, as a reminder of how much we have loved them and how deeply they are missed.

    Whatever your journey in life is, let it be one of adventure and know that when you least expect it, these perfect strangers will come into your life to give you of their bright light so that you can go on living life. I assure you that the meeting will be an unforgettable one. In this incarnation, these souls are not in your immediate circle, nor are you in theirs, yet the encounter takes place because there is no pending karma between you and having nothing to learn from one another all that is, is love and understanding even thought, apparently, we do not know each other. However, their essence is very familiar to us from the moment you meet and immediately we become attracted to them without knowing why.

    These souls know you well, and their job is to give you of their wisdom so that what needs to be understood, is finally understood. Once their job is done, they go back from whence they came, leaving you longing for their presence. These individuals are known as earth angels, they come in all sizes, shapes and colors and they have one thing in common; they give life a meaning that did not have before. You too are an 'earth angel' to others.

We should be grateful that we live in a universe that offers multiple possibilities, this assures us victory in every thing we do. We all came to Planet Earth well equipped to have a fruitful life. There are no mistakes in the universe and nothing happens by chance. To have a good life, allow the signs along the path to guide you. Know that you are never alone or are you left to wonder aimlessly in a desert of confusion because help and guidance are but a moment away.

The Contract of the Soul ~ Revised Edition 2011

Places and Things

"What you don't own, owns you.
What you don't understand confuses you.
Fear makes you weak."
Rev. Rina

A lesson is our Guardian Angel's and Mother Nature's way of teaching us to bring our energy to a higher level. A teacher can be everything; everyone, anywhere, and a lesson can be taught or learned at any time. Learning can be done at any age and the older the individual gets, the easier learning becomes. Have you noticed that anywhere you travel to, the place has its own particular energy? Could this energy be the energy of the people? Have you noticed that the locals earn their living selling the goods of their land? Have you noticed that in each people make things? Can it be possible that these objects or things hold the energy of the one who made it?

A place or a thing is a teacher, which comes to teach a lesson, perhaps the lesson of acceptance, so that we can finally learn to let go of biases and judgment. A teacher can be a song, a book, the sunset, daybreak, the words of a stranger, the smile in a child's face. A teacher can be the unexpected breeze that caresses your face. A teacher is whatever will take you to see that you are a spark of divinity and as part of God's Creation your time to awake has finally arrive.

Count the many teachers you have had in this lifetime and be grateful for having the opportunity of learn from such wonderful souls. Know that each lesson brings valuable tools. Think of the many times you have refused to learn your lessons and if this is the case, go back to that particular moment and learn the lesson willingly, loving learning it. Enjoy the teacher, the lesson, and the experience, knowing that your life will be better because you finally got out of the way of your own emancipation.

Rev. Rina A. González

"Religions are basically inventions of the human mind…Compassion is fundamental to our nature. To achieve it we do not need to become religious, nor do we need any ideology. All that is necessary is for us to bring forth our basic human qualities."

Dalai Lama

To err is divine

The mistakes in your life are covered in splendor
For they have within the seed that will bring
The unfoldment of self and a happier morrow
That without a mistake you might not foresee.

Be kind to yourself when you make a mistake.
Do not listen to those who claim to know all.
Follow your heartbeat; be true to your senses,
And let your source guide you to where you should be.

If err was as bad as we've made it to be
Why then would we need to learn anything?
Err is nature's ways of letting you know
That there is room for improvement,
And much need to grow.

Don't lose courage or weaken nor crumble,
For as dawn appears, darkness dissipates.
With every sunrise, you'll have a new canvas
Where life's treasures can joyfully be kept.

As the earl of haste comes making its way
Be gentle and poised in front of disgrace.
For when it is done, you will see that life happens
To those who are willing to be unafraid.

To err is divine for it has within it
The measure of life inside every stitch.
If you take the time to look at life's wonders,
You'd see that her fullness makes you be serene.

And as you make your way to a better morrow
You will see that you are erring less.
Life has that you know, you learn as you go.
So love every mistake you will ever make!

Rev. Rina A. González

The Contract of the Soul ~ Revised Edition 2011

Planet Earth

"Peace between countries must rest on the solid foundation of love between individuals."

Mahatma Gandhi

We refer to Planet Earth as our mother and I am happy to see that at least we have that right, for indeed, she is our mother. We not only have her nature but what is more important is that we are traveling through time and space on her back. We can even say that our relationship is a close one, so close that at time we loose sight of the fact that we are insignificants specs of nothingness traveling through the galaxy aboard our mother ship.

While getting her name right is a good start, what is incomprehensible to me is why we, her children, have abused our mother, when in reality, she is our only home? As children of a loving Father/Mother God, we should be more in tune with both our natures {soul and being}. Yet because of not recognizing both natures as one, our behavior has deteriorated making our collective state a deplorable one.

Love is much more than a simple word and unless used consciously, it is meaningless. People from all walks-of-life, use the word love and some even manage to sound sincere when using it. Yet, the condition of live on Planet Earth proves that too many, the word love has become a cordial form of solution, lacking the slightest reflection of who truly are.

To some of us love means feeling affection towards some one or some thing. To others, love is the need to have the presence of those we love constantly by our side. In trying to define the meaning of the word love, humans go as far as to say that they worship those they love. We even give names to the various love we feel and go as far as to put them in order of importance. Yet, as we change our minds about that person that was so important to us, we then say that we no longer feel love towards that person. So my question is; what you felt, what is unconditional love or love based on a condition?

We are love, we come from love. Not understanding who and what we are is what has created the deplorable state in which we find ourselves in. What is more amazing is that all the upheaval has come from thinking that indeed we love, when only its opposite is true. Not understanding what love means is why many of us say things like; 'My heart is broking'. Now I ask you; how can a muscle in the chest that grows and beats, ever break? The heart can and will malfunction, yet this is based on the persons nutritional habits. The heart can stop beating, but never can it break, that is an impossibility.

Love is being at peace with life itself. To love is being accepting of everything and everyone. To love is to hear the call of something greater than you. Love is felt, sensed, seen, and found in everything around you. Love comes in many forms. Love can be felt in the gentle breeze that caresses your face as in the sweet smile of a total stranger.

To love is to see life through the eyes of another person and accepting their view not as your own but as theirs. To love is having the courage to follow your dream and then share it with the world. To love is doing your part for the betterment of the whole of humanity.

Planet Earth, our mother, teaches us how to be humane. Yet our humanity has been compromised by our lack of reasoning. As a planet, she could very well throw us off her back. Fortunately, gravity keeps us safe for now. On the other hand, could it be that her motherly instinct has hope.

The Contract of the Soul ~ Revised Edition 2011

My greatest hope is that one day we'll come to terms with both our natures, and my greatest concern is that we won't.

Observe nature at work and see how everything grows and changes in perfect silence. From the power of creation comes the command to create, and in silence creation begins and all things are made a new under the powerful silence of love. And what do we do with such miracle? We tear down its perfection by creating wars, pollution, and devastation.

We are the rational mammal of the species and just because we walk up right and have five digits in hands and toes, think that we are superior. Has it ever occurred to you that our actions are inhumane? If you disagree, I am sorry to disappoint you but the truth is that we are. Perhaps it is time to reevaluate our actions, for they have contributed to the disharmony that all life form on our planet is, experiencing.

As I was saying, love is much more than saying the word, or thinking that because it is used, we possess it or express it. How can we give what we do not recognize or know we are? I know this to be true, because I see that our true essence has been compromised by our arrogance and our total disregard for life itself. If you think that what I say is my opinion, look around you and tell me if what you see, comes from love or from the lack thereof.

Our planet is full of our actions. What is even more telling is that our actions are full of fear, hate, ignorance, and greed. Seldom, is the energy of love strong enough, to sustain itself or be able to create beauty as it once did. We come from universal love, we are the embodiment of love. Yet in our confused state of mind, all we have managed to do, is devalue our worth.

Being detached from our reality keeps us in total disagreement with both our natures, reason why we cannot express our divinity or know how to feel love or can we give love. We do not know how to love, nor do we know how to live life. Our lack of tolerance and compassion towards each other is unjustifiable as is insane, reason why our relationships are in constant turmoil and are doomed to fail.

As a witness to our misconduct, see the need to let everyone know that unless we change our selfish greedy acts, we are doomed. Change is as inevitable as breathing is. Change is the ever-constant evolution of life. Life can be made a new at any given moment, all that is required for change to take place is for you to make the conscious choice to change so that change can come.

Man has two mothers, nature, and circumstances. From now on, depending on how each one of us uses our nature, either to benefit mankind, or to destroy life, we will be remembered as those who came together to change our world's circumstance or, as those who caused their own demise.

The Contract of the Soul ~ Revised Edition 2011

Yantra [symbol] of the Divine Feminine

"Womanhood"

*"How passionate can I be?
How many dreams can I have?
As much passion as my heart can hold
And as many dreams as I dare to envision."*

Rev. Rina

A woman is a symbol of greatness, for she possesses the fragrance of exquisite tenderness, encompassing the whole of humanity. Yes! Every woman is capable of being graceful, beautiful, courageous, powerful, and famous. Adored by those who know her, admired by those who seek her, and needed by those she loves. A woman embodies 'Mother Nature's wisdom, elegance and poise, yet at times, her powers are limited because she lacks knowing how to use them ineffective.

When she finds herself in the middle of a difficult situation, a woman can stand her ground and state her case. Seldom is a woman at a loss for words or have a problem letting others know exactly what is on her mind. Except, when she comes from a place of intolerance her powers are minimized and her credibility is lost. A woman is love personified and as such, she has Mother Nature's wisdom sketched in her soul. A woman loves passionately and when she is loved in return, she expresses her love in many different forms.

A woman can be patient and tolerant as well as being the one who impose the rules in the home or business. Above all a woman possesses the innate ability of listening to her inner voice and acts upon what she hears knowing that her moment has come to do what only she can do. A woman is a devoted friend who speaks her truth and is able to empower those around her with her words of wisdom. Whatever her age, whatever title she holds, every woman possess the secret of 'The Divine Feminine' within her womb. As the giver of life, her job is to guide and care for the young. And while her job is fulfilling, it is never done.

Part of a woman's job is to impart her wisdom on those she loves. A woman knows that inside every child there is a soul who needs to be recognized, nourished, understood, accepted, and loved. Our very essence demands that each one of us looks at what in our absence has taking place in our lives, in our communities, cities, country and in the entire world. It is time to reclaim our rightful place in society so that together we can bring love back to all life form on the planet. I feel this to be true for every woman on Planet Earth knowing that socially is what needs to happen. Unless, every woman takes it upon herself to make changes that will empower Planet Earth, every attempt made to have peace will fall short from achieving its full grace.

Women are powerful, magical goddesses who can do anything we set our minds to. Our greatest feat will be when we stand shoulder to shoulder with our counterparts and use our power of love to take back Mother Earth from the brink of extinction. As each woman reclaims her rightful place in society, we will free Our Mother from the hands of those who have abused her. We will heal her pain with our unconditional love, with our compassion, and with the light of our consciousness. This is how Mother Earth can be made strong again.

Rev. Rina A. González

The Contract of the Soul ~ Revised Edition 2011

Life is a Choice

The "secret" of the life that we are all looking for, is just this: to develop through sitting daily and by practicing the power and courage to return to that which we have spent a lifetime hiding from, to rest in the bodily experience of the present moment ~ even if it is a feeling of being humiliated, of failing, of abandonment, or of unfairness.

Charlotte Joko Beck

  I reincarnated by choice and by choice I am alive. After much to do about nothing, have come to see that life is a fascinating and an intriguing event that should be lived to its fullest. I also know that I found life's essence in the process of living my life. To me, life never gets old and every day is a new beginning. Life has always given me the desire to go onto a new adventure; as if somehow she had summoned me to discover her.

  As a fervent student of life, I do not want to stop learning, growing or evolving because see that my life changed the day I made the conscious decision to change and know that my greatest joy is seen my own transformation. Funny thing, while I do not remember signing up or agreeing to, many of the things that happened in my life, yet have finally understood that not liking the experience was what gave way to changing them.

  How did I become aware that there was another way of living my life? By not accepting what social conditioning dictates [the norm] and by asking the right questions, hearing the answers and acting upon what I have learned.

  I remember the day when I finally realized that life just **is,** and how this powerful force which, is in me and is all around me had never asked for my approval to be; it simple is. This was the moment when it became clear that to live life, all I have to do is get involved in my life. When I stopped taking the **'if's'** in life seriously and trusted the experiences for what each of them held, learned to accept my role as a confident witness. This newfound freedom took me to see the magic behind life's simplicity and her capacity to create something from nothing.

One thing lead to the other, and one day came across life's magic in her full splendor. It happened during meditation on day when I could see the light within me expand and become a spiral that traveled up my spine, awakening the charkas, as its multiple colors created harmony throughout my entire body.

As I observed the light expand, saw its intelligence, power, perfection, beauty, love, and grace and was pleased to learn that this magic **is** not only mine, what is more amazing is that this light, this power is truly who I am.

Then I came to see that this is what I had experienced when I was a child, yet not until that very moment had I understood the meaning or the importance in life. As I saw my light making life a new inside of me was when I understood that life begins at the core of our very existence and from here is that life blossoms. It is from the power of light that I am, that life began in the fetus, and it is from this light that a mass of nothingness became a human being. I had finally understood the immeasurable power, might, and dynamism, which creates such perfection in the silence of a womb, in rhythm with all that *is*.

For the first time since arriving on Planet Earth, I felt at peace with my creator, with my parents, with my children, with life and with myself. This state of bliss took me to see what my true purpose in life was and since that moment have worked on giving the best of what I have to offer.

Many things have happened since that day as well as knowing that many of my dreams have become real, yet know that what the writing of this book is my soul's purpose and I am overjoyed to have come this far in my journey as to make sense of what I lived and why.

Always saw myself writing a book that would take the reader away from the fallacies and myth of ignorance, confusion, and greed by shedding light or giving clarity with my words, if I have done that then I have remained faithful to my soul's purpose and another one of my wishes has come true.

I leave you with this. I am grateful for having been able to accomplished what I set out to do, as I am grateful for having come to experience life, for I finally see that in the process of living and experiencing life was that I was able to accomplish my soul's mission."

Rev. Rina A. González

The Contract of the Soul ~ Revised Edition 2011

Alpha and Omega

I am Alpha and Omega,
The Beginning and the End!
All starts with me in the sunlight
And ends with me in the rain.

I am light, love, and splendor
For all eyes to see and feel.
Close your eyes and you're in heaven
Dressed in silver, gold, and myrrh.

I am the powerful cry
That awakens all the senses.
I am the joy that's deep within
That inspires many races.

I am the Daughter of Earth
And the Goddesses of the Moon
With my powers in my hands
That comes from my Womanhood.

I am peace that comes from knowing
That my heart and mind are one,
United in its full splendor
Granting the peace that I am.

With my words I give you hope
And a peace that will abound,
As your senses are awaken
Taking you to higher grounds.

Rev. Rina A. González

You'll see Mercury arise
From the East wearing his gifts
As his three graces arrive
Dressed in rays of joy, and myth.

And as you feel their embrace
Praised be to their powerful might.
Fall in the love under the Moon
As you thank your Shining Star!

Final Thoughts

"The only reason why mankind has to find the way by which to evolve is to not to lose sight of what is real. The opposite of evolution is involution and if we continue doing what has brought us to this day, we will become an insignificant spec of nothingness scattered throughout space."

Every human being has the potential to do anything we want to do. Learn to use your spiritual gifts correctly, and in time, your decision to change your life will bring you great rewards.

By becoming a co-creator of your fate, the need to blame others ceases. Be accountable for your actions and this will take you to own your life. I promise you that if you do, you will never again suffer the consequences of an undetermined fate.

My sincere wish is that as you allow change to enter, your humanity, and your soul, become one.

Rev. Rina A. González

Rev. Rina A. González

Author's Work

Seminars, Workshops and Classes:

- Awakening the Goddess Within
- The 12 Universal Laws
- The Contract of the Soul Seminar

Books: Published and soon to be released:

The Contract of the Soul	2008
An Everlasting Love ~ My Father's Poetry	2010
The Contract of the Soul ~ Revised Edition	2011
CUBA: Resurrecting the Amethyst Isle	2011
The 12 Universal Laws	2012
Reaching Unana, the Consciousness of One	2012
Provocative & Serene ~ Poetry	2012
"Destiny" ~ Chronicles of a Legacy	2013

www.ingramcontent.com/pod-product-compliance
Lightning Source LLC
Chambersburg PA
CBHW070455100426
42743CB00010B/1633